A Parent's Guide
to Prayer

KATHY HENDRICKS

A Parent's Guide to Prayer

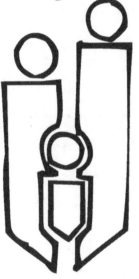

TWENTY-THIRD PUBLICATIONS

185 WILLOW STREET • PO BOX 180 • MYSTIC, CT 06355
TEL: 1-800-321-0411 • FAX: 1-800-572-0788
Bayard E-MAIL: ttpubs@aol.com • www.twentythirdpublications.com

Credits

Excerpt from *Prayers for the Domestic Church*, by Edward M. Hays, ©1999. Used with permission of the publisher, all rights reserved. Forest of Peace publishing, an imprint of Ave Maria Press, Notre Dame, IN 46556-0428; www.avemaria-press.com.

Excerpt from *Catholic Household Blessings and Prayers*, ©1989. Used with permission of the United States Conference of Catholic Bishops, Washington, DC.

The Scripture passages contained herein are from the *New Revised Standard Version of the Bible*, Catholic Edition, copyright ©1989, by the Division of Christian Education of the National Council of the Churches of Christ in the U.S.A. Used by permission. All rights reserved.

Twenty-Third Publications
A Division of Bayard
185 Willow Street
P.O. Box 180
Mystic, CT 06355
(860) 536-2611 or (800) 321-0411
www.twentythirdpublications.com
ISBN:1-58595-348-2

Library of Congress Catalog Card Number: 2004106801
Printed in the U.S.A.copyright

Dedication

To my parents, Margaret and Albert
who taught me more about prayer than they ever knew

Contents

Introduction

Picture this…A family gathers around a table. Heads bowed and hands folded they begin to pray, calmly and quietly thanking God for the food that is laid out before them in perfect order.

It makes a lovely picture. It just isn't real—for most of us, that is.

Where is the scowling teenager? The toddler who has just upended a bowl of peas? The phone jangling in the background or the carpool van blaring its horn outside the front door? It's challenging enough for families to sit down together for a meal these days. Tacking on a quiet and peaceful experience seems next to impossible.

When I set out to write a book on family prayer, I wanted to make it usable for today's parent. I reviewed books on the same topic and found many to be helpful, some outdated, and others too narrowly focused on families with young children.

I also polled groups of parents and religious educators, asking what they would seek in such a book. Their responses were both surprising and predictable. Parents wanted a book that would be realistic about who families are, what they do, and how much time they have together. Some expressed their desire to know more about teaching their children to pray, especially during times of

1

crises. Terrorist attacks, economic downturns, sniper shootings, and child abductions were some of the events peppering the news at that time. Parents were painfully aware of the anxieties and fears with which their children lived on a daily basis. How, they asked, can we help them pray in such frightening and uncertain times?

Religious educators noted the need for practical materials that help parents learn about the what, why, where, and how of prayer, first for themselves and then for their families. They also wanted a resource that could be used in their churches as a basis for understanding the possibilities and practicalities of domestic prayer.

A Parent's Guide to Prayer has a threefold purpose. First, it is meant to help parents deepen their understanding, knowledge, and experience of prayer as applied to their own lives. This is especially important as parents feel the dual realities of too much responsibility and too little time weighing upon them.

It is difficult, if not impossible, to teach what we don't know. When parents are prayerful, they can be both model and mentor for their children. The book's second purpose is to serve as a guide for teaching children how to pray as they pass through various stages of development, from infancy through adolescence.

Third, the book offers ideas and suggestions for praying together as a family. This does not necessarily mean involving each household member in every communal experience. Family prayer ranges from everyone gathered around a table together to a parent seated by a child's bedside, helping with a nighttime blessing. Therefore, various configurations of "family" are presented as a way to keep the concept of domestic prayer from becoming too narrowly defined.

Each chapter ends with a section called Our Family. It contains questions, reflections, or activities that readers can adapt and apply to their household's particular needs, interests, and circumstances.

A Walk through the Book

A Parent's Guide to Prayer begins with the basics of prayer—its value in family life, what it is, and the different expressions and forms that it takes. It then moves to the where of prayer and examines the need to set aside both external and internal space in which to pray. The rhythm of prayer follows, with a look at how it can be woven into the fabric of daily routines, seasonal rituals, and the unexpected twists and turns that accompany domestic life.

Not all prayer comes easily. Time constraints and distractions, grief and loss, trouble and stress, or just plain laziness can beset even the most ardent pray-er. Ways to transform these situations into opportunities for growth are presented in a chapter on the challenge of prayer. Lastly, a plan for keeping spiritually fit is offered as a way to maintain a strong and healthy practice of prayer.

This book is not the definitive word on prayer in the home. Quite the contrary. It is a starting point for some parents, offering encouragement and motivation. For others it will serve as an affirmation of what they are already doing and provide fresh insights into both personal and communal spirituality. In all cases, parents will want to draw upon the ideas and inspiration that fit their personalities and preferences, circumstances and experiences. These are the ones they are most likely to share with their children.

A sampling of favorite prayers is sprinkled throughout the book and a list of resources is provided in the appendix. My hope is that it will encourage interest in compiling a home-based library that will nurture both parent and child in a lifelong pattern of prayer and reflection.

CHAPTER 1

What Good Is Prayer?

The family that prays together, stays together. This saying has been around for years. It's a pleasant thought but not altogether accurate. The truth is that there are families who, despite their grace-saying habits, have split apart. On the other hand, families who have never uttered a prayer, together or individually, have remained intact.

What good, then, is prayer for a family? We might approach this question by looking first at what it won't do for us. It is not a magic bullet, one that zeroes in on every need and foible, fixing each one so that life proceeds happily ever after. On the contrary, prayer may raise more questions than it answers. It may make us more aware of hurt and pain and suffering rather than shielding us from them. It can disturb, stimulate, and create dissonance. And all of this, if we have the tenacity to stick with it, ultimately brings us closer—to God and to one another.

Here is another old saying: "Prayer doesn't change God, it changes us." This may be the single most important thing to know about prayer—its transformative power. Becoming a parent is a life-changing event that draws us out of self-absorption. We are suddenly responsible for the upbringing, care, and guidance of another human being. It is a terrifying, wondrous, perplexing experience, one that changes focus just as we think we have a handle on who this person—our child—is. Quite simply, we need all the help we can get.

In the midst of a crisis or transition, it is easy to lose a sense of perspective. Prayer at such times can ground us, calm us, and bring us a broader point of view, one that reminds us that, in time, "this, too, shall pass." If, as a mother, I have learned anything about the value of prayer, it is that God will be with me, no matter what. That knowledge alone has gotten me through more than one harried day or rest-less night. It has given me hope.

The Family Circle

There is movement in family life. Our children venture outward into school and peer groups, eventually leaving us for families, careers, and lives of their own. As the circle expands and contracts, the involvement of household members in communal prayer does too. Teens may be absent, physically because of their involvement with school, sports, friends, and jobs, or emotionally because of their moods and attitudes. While the latter can be disturbing to the parent who has tried to make faith a central part of family life, it is also a natural part of a child's growth. Family prayer goes with the flow, taking place with whoever happens to be present.

While there are commonalities, each household is unique in its approach to the cycles of life. Because of this, a single style of prayer cannot fit all families. It can't even fit one! It is challenging to maintain a prayer routine as schedules tighten and circumstances shift. The different ages and stages that make domestic life so fluid require a variety of forms and expressions of prayer. So, too, does meeting the needs, interests, and comprehension levels of toddlers, young children, preteens, adolescents, and adults. In time, we learn how to adapt, making prayer both an intentional activity and a spontaneous event. Parents need knowledge and understanding of the breadth and possibility of prayer, along with opportunities to put it into practice. In the end, however, life itself creates the context for prayer, drawing it in and out of us as we strive and struggle to stay committed to one another and to our faith.

Snapshots

One of my favorite photographs was taken at the time of my son's graduation from college. The four of us—my husband, daughter, son, and I—are seated on a couch in a hotel lobby. Each looks relaxed and close-knit as we nestle together. The graduation ceremony that convened us in lower Manhattan had come after a spate of trying and difficult years. Our family had weathered some terrible storms, including a painful miscarriage, devastating job loss, and two interstate moves. At one point, when I was feeling most discouraged, my son reassured me: "We are a strong family and we will get through this." Sitting together on that couch, I knew the verity of his words. The picture took on new significance when, a few months later, the hotel was destroyed in the September 11, 2001, attack on the World Trade Center.

Prayer had played a strong part in holding us together in the days, weeks, and years leading up to that moment. While our family was miles apart—a son in New York and a daughter in

Arizona—we were bound together in spirit. Every laugh shared and tear shed, every hug and headache had been part of that experience, all of it sewn together by faith, buoyed by hope, and fueled by love.

The family that prays together, _____ together.

I have been trying to create a succinct restatement about what prayer does for families as a summation of this chapter. In truth, there isn't a single way to frame it. Rather, it is a fill-in-the-blank exercise, one that changes as the family does, sometimes from minute to minute, and other times from one generation to the next. Prayer helps families grow, cry, laugh, learn, and question together. My family photo shows me that it also helps us believe, hope, and love together. Perhaps that is what its "staying" power is all about.

Guiding Your Child

As every parent knows, children grow up. Just as they move through various stages of physical, mental, and emotional development, they also pass through spiritual ones. Understanding these stages can help parents teach children to pray in ways that are consistent with their capacities at the various ages and stages of their lives.

In their book, *Circle of Grace*, parents Gregory and Suzanne M. Wolfe write that prayer ideally begins before a child is born or adopted. They write, "What better way to give expression to all the hopes and longings of expectant parents than through the medium of prayer?" After a baby's arrival, prayer can be an immersion in which parents surround their child with lullabies, blessings, and petitions that invoke God's care and protection.

As they move into early childhood, children pick up the rhythm of prayer when they start to recognize the wonder of God's presence in their surroundings. At this point their faith is dependent on that of others, especially their parents. The laying of a foundation for prayer at this stage has obvious benefits. Parents can guide their children by speaking in simple terms about the ways God helps, loves, and cares for us. All of these are comforting images for children as well as ones that lay a foundation for believing in God's power and presence.

When children enter school, their world expands. While parents are still the primary influence in their lives, children start to discover and develop friendships and to relate to other adults and authority figures. At this stage, they think in concrete terms. "Their assumption [is] that God is a person, someone to whom they can talk and relate" (Wolfe and Wolfe). They can learn short prayers and may be the initiators of mealtime grace and simple blessings. This is a good stage in which to invite their observations about God, faith, and going to church. Their insight often astounds us with its innate wisdom and simplicity of vision. As they continue to grow, so, too, does their capacity for empathy. Thus their prayers can move beyond personal need in order to include others, especially those who are suffering.

As children enter adolescence, their peer relationships take on increased importance. Outside influences or inner turmoil might draw them away from formal participation in church or the family circle of prayer. This can be an alarming stage for parents who may fear that their child is losing his faith. It is actually a normal phase, signifying the need to "own" one's faith through questioning and perhaps by even rejecting the religious practice and belief of the parent. In turn, adolescents may be seeking a spiritual friendship, one in which God is like "a person who can ride out the bumps with them, who will understand the good they do and the problems they get themselves into" (Patricia H. Davis, *Beyond Nice: The Spiritual Wisdom of Adolescent Girls*).

At this stage parents can provide their children with resources that foster reflection and that pose and answer questions. Journaling may be a useful way for preteens and teens to express themselves in writing, thus giving voice to their hopes, fears, questions, frustrations, and concerns. Student bibles designed for adolescents include prefaces with issues related to contemporary life and easy-to-decipher guidelines for reading Scripture.

Family Prayer

There are two natural ways to pray together which are especially helpful for those just starting out or in households with young children. Grace before or after meals is simple and understandable to one and all. Families can use a traditional blessing or make it spontaneous. Responsibility for leading grace might rest with a parent or pass from one person to the next. It is a time-honored practice that nurtures a spirit of gratitude, provides a focal point for the meal, and binds a family together.

A more intimate occasion for prayer is bedtime. It marks a soothing transition from activity to rest and provides a way to review the day's happenings within the perspective of faith. For children afraid of the dark, prayers that bespeak of God's loving presence bring comfort and reassurance. The whole family might set aside five minutes in which to turn off the television, light a candle, and share a short reading and blessing. Because bedtime rituals are simple, they are easy to maintain, in some form, throughout the cycle of family life.

Our Family

Given our family's current circumstances, how would I/we complete this statement about prayer?

The family that prays together, _____ together.

Pick out a favorite snapshot of your family and discuss these questions together:

- What brought us together for the picture?
- What keeps us together?
- What does the picture tell about our family's "staying power"?
- How is God a part of our life as a family? Of my life as a parent?

A Prayer for a Family

We are a family.
For one another,
  we are love and trial,
  strength and trouble.
Even when far apart,
  we belong to one another and,
  in various ways,
  we remember and pray for one another.
                    — Catholic Household Blessings and Prayers

CHAPTER 2

Getting Down to Basics

What Every Parent Needs
to Know About Prayer

Prayer is often defined as talking and listening to God. This rather basic description contains two of prayer's important characteristics. The first is that it is both an active and a passive process. We name our needs, hopes, desires, fears, and frustrations, trusting that God will hear them. There comes a time, however, when we must stop and listen, waiting for what is hidden to be revealed. This is not an overnight process. It takes time—God's time—and so we must cultivate the virtue of patience and exercise the practice of attentiveness.

The talking/listening aspect of prayer reveals its second important characteristic, namely, that it is relational. We are not tossing our petitions out into some faceless, cosmic void, but towards Someone who listens and answers, even if we are unable to fully understand the response. Prayer is an expression of our faith in God's presence. "It is a doorway into heaven on earth. It can open and clear our eyes and ears, quicken our heart, and deepen our mindfulness, so that we may more easily discern where heaven lives in this moment, in this place" (Wayne Muller, *Learning to Pray*).

As a parent, I have relied heavily upon the hope and comfort that such prayer brings. In so doing, I have followed in the footsteps of countless mothers and fathers who have known the same kind of uncertainty, confusion, wonder, heartache, and joy that I have.

The Prayer of the Parent

At some level, often beneath my awareness, I never stop muttering to God. —Nancy Mairs

When I was growing up my parents often turned to a group of Carmelite nuns to ask for their prayers when things reached a critical point in our family. The practice both intrigued and puzzled me. On the one hand, it was a sign of my parents' faith in the power of prayer and their recognition that they needed the help of others—the "professionals," so to speak. On the other hand, I questioned why our prayers as a family weren't good enough. Wouldn't God listen just as intently to my mother as to a Mother Superior?

Although parents are not usually quoted as the experts, there is ample evidence of the power their prayers held over the course of Judeo-Christian history, particularly in the Bible. In it, we find many examples of mothers and fathers entreating God for a child who would be a sign of blessing, a way to carry on from one generation to the next.

In the Book of Genesis, Abraham spills out his anguish over Sarah's infertility, even after God promises him many rewards. "O Lord God, what will you give me, for I continue childless...?" (Genesis 15:2). God, in response, takes him outside, instructs him to examine the sky, and promises to make his descendants as numerous as the stars.

In the Book of Samuel, Hannah longs so fervently for a child that she vows to give him right back to God. After her prayer is answered, she fulfills her part of the bargain by taking her son, Samuel, to the temple and placing him in the care of Eli, the priest. (1Samuel 2).

Two of the most stunning expressions of parental prayer appear in the Gospel of Luke. Mary, after listening to the angelic announcement of her impending motherhood, responds with a magnificent prayer of praise (Luke 1:46–55). Zechariah, who is struck dumb by news of his wife's pregnancy, rejoices after Elizabeth gives birth to John (Luke 1:67–79). Both of these prayers have a permanent place in the Christian Liturgy of the Hours as profound expressions of praise for God's power and goodness.

Parents give voice to prayer through the flow of both the large and small events of family life: the wonder that follows the birth of a baby. The gratitude that accompanies the realization of a long-awaited adoption. The blessing of a toddler after the third attempt at getting him to bed. The entreaties for forgiveness after an explosive argument with a willful twelve-year-old. The midnight petitions for a teenager's safe return from the prom. "Muttering to God" is an experience to which many parents can relate.

Without being conscious of it, parents already know a great deal about various ways to pray because they have already been putting them into practice. To strengthen these efforts, however, it is helpful to deepen our understanding and appreciation of the form, expression, and language that prayer involves. In doing so we make prayer more intentional and teach our children to do the same.

Ways to Pray—Five Forms of Christian Prayer

Petition

We have confused God with Santa Claus.—Rabbi Harold Kushner

At some point in my Catholic schooling, a teacher told me that, if I prayed for something between the raising of the host and the chalice during Mass, I would be sure to receive it. While this has never been a teaching of the Church, it opened up for me something akin to a spiritual wishing well and I began to pray fervently for my heart's greatest desire—a Tiny Tears doll. My prayer was answered when the doll appeared, like magic, under our tree on Christmas morning. I had indeed mixed God up with Santa Claus.

When teaching his disciples how to pray, Jesus told them, "Ask, and it will be given you" (Matthew 7:7). This forms the basis for prayers of petition. We lay our deepest needs before God, ones that become less evident as life grows more complex. We then might follow the example of Buddhist monks. Because, at one time, they were not permitted to keep food overnight, they went out each day with a begging bowl. Whatever was placed in it would meet their needs for the day. This formed their "daily bread." So it should be for us.

In our over-abundant culture how do we know what is enough? The prayer of petition leaves that up to God. Sometimes we get the doll under the tree. Other times we receive something unexpected, perhaps even unwanted, that turns out to be exactly what we need.

At times our deepest need is for healing. Therefore it makes sense that petition includes entreaties for forgiveness. Such prayer reminds us that we are intricately connected. Nowhere is this felt more dramatically than in families where we acquire a knack for irritating each other, unleashing our frustrations upon one another, and sustaining our grudges far past the point when they should matter. Asking to forgive and to be forgiven is a way to seek peace, wholeness, and a restoration of relationships. It is prayer that changes the heart.

Blessing and Adoration

When we bless someone, we touch the unborn goodness in them and wish it well. —Rachel Naomi Remen

A form of prayer that we may have learned in early childhood is that of blessing. It might have been introduced to us as we gathered around the table and prayed over our food. We may have learned to make the Sign of the Cross as benediction was pronounced at the end of Mass. Perhaps our father or mother tucked us in bed and offered a prayer for our safe and secure night's sleep. Or we simply sneezed and received a handful of "bless you's" from the people within earshot.

In her book, *My Grandfather's Blessings*, Rachel Naomi Remen writes about learning this form of prayer from her grandfather, a Jewish rabbi. He tells her that in the Kaballah, the mystical teachings of Judaism, blessings are a way of coming in touch with God. "At some point in the beginning of things, the Holy was broken into countless sparks, which were scattered throughout the universe." Everyone and everything contains a "God spark." It is up to us to listen to how these sparks may speak to us within the ordinary parts of our days. One way to acknowledge such encounters is by invoking a blessing. Each one is considered a "moment of mindfulness" in which we take note of the sacred that surrounds us.

To receive or bestow a blessing is an act of tenderness. It affirms the love we have been given and that we have for others and for God. When we say that God has "blessed" us, it is not the same as having received some bit of good luck. Instead, we acknowledge that we are held in God's heart, cherished for who we are rather than for what we do, say, or possess. Blessing others "lights the spark" within them and brings into greater focus the ever-present reality of God.

Someone once described prayer as a "valentine to God." When offering prayers of blessing we express our adoration for God—an unabashed devotion for the One who gives and sustains life.

Another definition of prayer describes it as "stroking the face of God." It suggests an image of overwhelming affection and makes us as single-hearted as the most ardent lover.

Thanksgiving

Every time we remember to say "thank you" we experience nothing less than Heaven on earth. —Sarah Ban Breathnach

It is a short step from blessing and adoration to thanksgiving. It is also a natural one. The more we become aware of the "god sparks" within and around us, the more inclined we are to express our gratitude. Little children are especially adept at this form of prayer. Ask any Kindergarten teacher what happens when she invites her class to name the things for which they are grateful. The list grows endless as children identify everything from Grandpa to goldfish.

As we mature, the habit of giving thanks tends to shrink rather than enlarge. Perhaps it atrophies when we fall out of the habit of expressing our gratitude. We live in a culture of entitlement in which we expect to be given what is our "due." Such a milieu kills any inclination to be grateful for what we have; it only demands more.

A few years ago, I moved with my family to another state where I began an exciting new job. Before leaving, some friends gave me a gratitude journal. After getting settled, I took it out and started to make my daily entries. The year evolved into a long and painful ordeal, beset by loneliness, disappointment, and loss. Some days it was a struggle to name a single thing for which to be thankful. Maintaining the journal helped me weather that stormy period. I learned that there is always something for which to be grateful, even if it is as insignificant as a pansy peeking through a patch of weeds. Being thankful heightens our awareness and changes our perspective. It is a form of prayer that lifts us out of the darkness and into the light.

Praise

All creation teaches us some way of prayer. —Thomas Merton

"Fear of the Lord" is one of the seven gifts of the Holy Spirit. We commonly associate fear with being afraid but this is not an accurate way to define the Spirit's gift. Instead, it denotes awe, reverence, and an acknowledgment that we will never be able to fully grasp the magnificence of God.

We live in a culture in which informality is the norm and irreverence is considered hip. The latter manifests itself in the media as family, religion, and other traditional institutions are made targets for unrelenting satire. Being reverent in such an environment can seem hopelessly old-fashioned and naïve.

As one dives deeply into spiritual waters, however, awe and reverence saturate the soul. Witnessing a gilded sunset or studying the intricacies of a spider's web may extract from us a simple prayer of praise that is equivalent to an alleluia—"Wow!" Reverence and awe are replete in the psalms, prayers that are meant to be sung rather than said. Whether it is praising God for the wonder of heaven and earth (Psalm 148) or marveling at the divine artistry that is embodied in each of us (Psalm 139), these poetic masterpieces impel us to kick up our heels in joy.

Intercession

The Spirit helps us in our weakness; for we do not know how to pray as we ought, but that very Spirit intercedes with sighs too deep for words.
—Romans 8:26

My daughter, Jenny, died when she was just a year old. In the days, weeks, and months following her death I wandered around in a haze of anguish and grief. My thoughts and emotions were so jumbled that I didn't know what or how to pray. When others offered to pray "for" me I took it to heart, trusting that their prayers would carry me through that tumultuous time. In some mysterious way they did.

I also experienced first-hand what Paul described as the Spirit praying in "sighs" that could not be expressed in speech. The keening of my heart was terrifying in its magnitude. I have since been able to recognize how God held me, weeping with and for me and making what was unthinkable into something that eventually became bearable.

To intercede means to "ask on behalf of." As a Christian community, we offer General Intercessions at Mass, praying for leaders in our church and our world, for those who are suffering as a result of illness, grief, or injustice, and for those who have died. These are potent prayers, raised on behalf of those who need our collective strength.

In the Catholic tradition, we approach Mary and the saints as intercessors. As such, we do not pray "to" them, which is a common misperception about Catholic practice. Instead, we ask for their prayers on our behalf.

Over the centuries, saints have been named patrons and protectors, interceding for those with specific needs and guiding those with particular professions. It used to be commonplace, whether you were Catholic or not, to hang St. Christopher medals in the car, and ask him, as the patron saint of travelers, for his prayers. Statues of St. Francis of Assisi are placed in gardens as testimony to his great love of nature, and his feast day, October 4, is an occasion in many Christian churches to offer a blessing of animals.

Praying for another is a profound way to expand our spiritual horizons beyond our own needs and wants. It reminds us that we are interrelated and that what happens to one of us is felt, in some way, by all. When offered for others, such prayer increases our capacity for compassion. When others pray for us we draw upon their strength and are reminded that we are not meant to go it alone. And we can always rely on the Spirit to be praying with and for us when we cannot do it for ourselves.

The Language of Prayer

For me, prayer is a surge of the heart, it is a simple look turned toward heaven, it is a cry of recognition and of love, embracing both trial and joy. —St. Thérèse of Lisieux

Thérèse's description of prayer goes beyond "talking and listening." It illustrates the different types of language that prayer involves, ones rooted in the heart and using speech, song, and gesture to give voice to that which lies deep within us.

Words

My husband, Ron, collects quotes. He has them written on the walls of his darkroom and scribbled on pieces of paper stuck into books. The turn of a phrase by someone who is both thoughtful and eloquent inspires him. He is so fond of recalling his favorite quotes that, after saying the first one or two words, our children finish the line for him.

Words have power. They contain symbolism and meaning. Putting words together can be a poetic process, as attested to by some of our most cherished prayers—the Our Father, the Magnificat, the Serenity Prayer. Using the words of others—from the Bible, liturgy, or writings of saints, scholars, poets, and practitioners—is a revered way to pray. Such prayer lifts the heart in a surge of love and longing that comforts and reassures us. Likewise, the use of simple chants—words put together in rhythmic fashion—can calm and steady us, moving us into a state of receptivity and readiness to listen.

We bring our own words to prayer, too, and they are just as precious as those of the poet. Such words spring to heart and mind as we engage in the different forms of prayer, expressing our gratitude and awe, our remorse and requests, our love and concern for others. And, when we are at a loss for what might be the "right" words, we can be reassured by Paul's reminder that the Spirit prays for us in language we do not yet know or understand.

Music

My son, Eric, loves music. I never quite know what to expect when he sends us a CD of a newly discovered artist. His tastes are eclectic, ranging from blues and jazz to Celtic and classical. As a film editor, he appreciates music's potential for setting the mood and extending the storytelling beyond the actor's lines and camera's angle.

Music is the language of prayer that hums continually beneath the mundane aspects of life. The hymn "How Can I Keep From Singing" expresses this by extolling the ability of music to keep us steady as it raises an "echo" in our souls, lifting us above daily tumult and strife. With such wondrous background music how then we can we do anything but sing?

Music's language contains melodies, rhythms, and cadences that express all range of emotion. St. Augustine acknowledged this when he observed that to sing was to "pray twice." Whether it is joining in a cherished hymn or listening to a favorite composer, music offers a way to pray that does indeed raise us above the lamentations that are part of our earthbound lives.

Gesture

When our children were small, my husband and I joined with two other families to create a small community of faith. It was another way to pray as a family and with others. Our daughter, Anna, was especially fond of these gatherings and the interactive approach to prayer that they entailed. Much to our surprise, she started collecting all of the prayer sheets and art activities we used. It was clear that she found movement and social interaction a meaningful way to pray.

Various religious traditions use the whole body in prayer by standing, sitting, kneeling, bowing, dancing, and processing. When coupled with a symbolic action, such as lighting a candle or making the Sign of the Cross, a single gesture expresses what words cannot. Our "home church" gatherings included a liberal use of symbolic movement and activity. It kept everyone aware of the significance of our prayers and made them both relevant and engaging.

In his book, *Pray All Ways*, Edward Hays describes prayer as a process that "involves the entire body in an act of communion with the Divine Mystery." As a "whole body" experience, worship takes on a different feel when we raise our arms or drop to our knees. In the gospels, there are numerous examples of the gestures Jesus used when praying. When healing people, he placed his hands upon them as he prayed (Luke 4:40). During his agonizing night in the Garden of Gethsemane, he fell prostrate in grief (Matthew 26:39). Such gestures are an indication of how absorbed he was in prayer and of the communion he continually shared within the Divine Mystery.

For parents, gesture may accompany prayer without any conscious thought given to it. Worry or stress may cause us to wring our hands. Getting a piece of good news or celebrating a special occasion may spur a "high five" of sorts. Each gives voice to prayer that says as much by what we do as by what we say.

Expressions of Prayer

Prayer is the raising of one's mind and heart to God.

—St. John Damascene

Here is another classic definition of prayer. It notes the dual tasks of thinking and feeling and alludes to the need for both talking and listening. These are drawn out in three major expressions of prayer: vocal, meditative, and contemplative.

Vocal Prayer: Talking It Out

The words of prayer can be as simple as the request for a kitten or as grand as the great Amen of Easter. —Kristen Johnson Ingram

We vocalize our prayer in numerous ways—through speaking, chanting, writing, singing, crying, muttering, laughing, shouting, whispering...the list goes on and on. There is a need deep to give expression to the thoughts in our heads and the emotions in our hearts. For parents, the vocalizing of prayer emanates from the daily concerns and demands of raising children. We may not need to know more ways to talk to God; instead we may want to become appreciative of how constant and varied that dialogue is.

Meditation: Clearing the Mind

Be still, and know that I am God! —Psalm 46:10

If talking to God comes easily for a parent, listening is far more difficult. The practice of meditation entails periods of silence in which we make a concentrated effort to seek a greater understanding of God and of our faith. "We can meditate by pausing to reflect on what's going on, bringing our faith to discern what is or is not of God's reign, what the Spirit may be inviting, and how to respond in a faith-filled way" (Thomas H. Groome, *What Makes Us Catholic: Eight Gifts for Life*).

Sustained attentiveness of this kind is difficult in a monastery so we needn't worry if we can't perfect it in the living room. Reading a short passage from the Bible or a book on spirituality can help us to focus. Such activity lifts us out and away from daily distractions and offers us something to think about other than bills, schedules, and who's fighting over the remote control. This makes meditation a welcome respite for every parent.

Contemplation: Resting in God

Behind every blade of grass stands an angel telling it to grow.

—Hasidic saying

In her book, *Dance of the Spirit,* Maria Harris uses the examples of two mothers, one pregnant and the other nursing her baby, to illustrate the discipline of contemplation. Each one, she says, has achieved a stillness without being conscious of it. They are both in touch, through the experience of motherhood, with the Divine Mystery.

Thomas Merton, a Trappist monk famous for his prolific writing on spirituality, defined contemplation as a "loving sense of this life and this presence and this eternity." Rather than being attainable only for monks and nuns, contemplation is an expression of prayer that weaves itself into the normal experiences of family life. It calls for the cultivation of attentiveness to where we are and what we are doing. As such it provides us a way to pray without words, cultivating a "surge of the heart" and an opening of vision that enables us to see angels in the backyard and God's smile twinkling in our child's eyes.

Guiding Your Child

A simple way to explain prayer to young children is through use of the "talking and listening" definition. Expand their understanding of the talking part by pointing out that this includes speaking, thinking, singing, and other expressions of vocal prayer. Encourage times of quiet by taking brief pauses when praying together.

The five forms of prayer can be introduced early in a child's life. It is fairly simple to be aware of these forms and then make use of them as part of everyday rituals. Small children find it easy to name the things they want (petition). Parents can cultivate gratitude, awe, and reverence by drawing attention to the wonder and gifts that are part of daily life. Children, in turn, are often natural contemplatives and end up showing adults the way to pray at unexpected times and in curious places.

As they mature, children can be taught to memorize short and simple prayers, such as grace before meals and bedtime blessings. The Lord's Prayer is the most important prayer for Christians to know by heart. It is an essential part of communal worship as well as a personal meditation that grows in meaning with time. When teaching children to memorize prayers, it is helpful to tackle longer ones a sentence or phrase at a time. Such prayers stay with us for a lifetime, like cherished friends who are always there when we need them.

Utilize the Bible for prayer, especially as children learn to read. If this is an unfamiliar practice, purchase a study edition that offers notes on how to look up passages and provides background information. The Psalms contain a rich treasury of prayers that can be used with children and as a family. If your child is enrolled in a religious education class or attends parochial school, take advantage of prayer resources suggested by teachers or sent home as part of family activity components. Ask your child to teach the family songs learned in their classes as a way to incorporate music into family worship.

As children approach adolescence, their self-consciousness increases, often causing them worry and anxiety. Encourage them to bring their concerns to God and remind them that the answers to our prayers may not be what we expect. Music is a good outlet for children at this age, so expose them to a wide variety of styles and artists. Help them to overcome some of their self-consciousness by encouraging them to pray for others, especially those who are suffering. Their capacity for empathy is likely to be enlarged through such practice. Remind them that prayer has the greatest potential to change ourselves, expanding our vision in order to see others in a more compassionate and forgiving light.

It takes time and patience to teach children to pray. Therefore, set realistic expectations for yourself and your family. If daily prayer is something new, for example, don't start out with an extended meditation. Likewise, it is best to be flexible and forgiving. Expect some silliness and sullenness and remind yourself frequently that learning to pray is more of a process than a plan. Keep in mind that the word "disciple" comes from the same root word as that of "discipline." The latter should be viewed as a virtue to be practiced rather than a punishment to be endured. And, as with anyone who is striving to become a better artist or athlete, discipline requires regularity, repetition, and dedication.

Our Family

Take an assessment of your family's prayer life by discussing the following questions together or with a spouse:

- How do we pray together?
- How would we like to pray together?
- What more would we like to know about prayer?
- Where can we go to find answers?

Prayer of Saint Francis

Lord, make me an instrument of your peace:
where there is hatred, let me sow love;
where there is injury, pardon;
where there is doubt, faith;
where there is despair, hope;
where there is darkness, light;
where there is sadness, joy.
O Divine Master, grant that I may not so much seek
to be consoled as to console,
to be understood as to understand,
to be loved as to love.
For it is in giving that we receive,
it is in pardoning that we are pardoned,
and it is in dying that we are born to eternal life.

CHAPTER 3

The Where of Prayer

I grew up on Ivy Lane. It was a small semi-circular street that looped off a parkway and then made its way back again. As such, it didn't lead anywhere. Its primary function was to bring people home.

Our house was situated at the top of the street's arch. It was the second dwelling built on the block, designed by an architect and close friend of my parents. Constructed prior to the start of World War II, our family lived there for thirty-two years. For the first nineteen years of my life it was my sole experience of home.

It was a beautiful house. The Tudor architecture, expansive lawn, rose garden, and ivy vines made it both stately and cozy. Large enough to accommodate crowds of people, it was the focal point for all of our family gatherings. My five siblings and numerous relatives made these quite boisterous so I soon learned to seek out the quiet spaces. Nooks and crannies, such as the child-sized "toy" closets, became favorite places to be alone. It was the beginning of a lifelong appreciation of solitude and an understanding that both interior and exterior spaces are necessary for prayer.

The where of prayer has long been a critical concern for religious institutions. Over the centuries, extensive planning, resources, and creativity have been devoted to the design of churches and cathedrals, shrines and synagogues, mosques and monasteries. In recent days, there has been renewed interest in the practice of feng shui. Derived from an ancient Chinese art, it involves careful attention to the interaction of energy with objects, places, and people.

While this might sound a tad complicated for the average family, the principle behind it is important. Our physical environment matters. Not only does it provide the ambience conducive to various practices of prayer, but it also reminds us of the need to be diligent about our spiritual lives. Like Ivy Lane, it brings us home and helps us to discover internal space in which to rest in God's grace and abundant love.

When I polled parents about their interest in this book, the "where" of prayer ranked lowest on the list of potential topics. It was surprising because space seems to be a major issue in family life today. Parents need to establish room, both external and internal, in their lives for prayer and teach their children to do the same.

Creating Exterior Space for Prayer

In his classic book, *Prayers for the Domestic Church*, Edward Hays notes the need for each of us to locate "holy space." We might find it, he says, "in a den, a bedroom, or even a basement."

I once asked a group of women where they go to pray. They responded with a lovely blend of whimsy and practicality. Some found quiet refuge in the bathroom where they could shut out the rest of the household. Others named a piece of furniture, such as a rocking chair or kitchen table as a favorite place to sit and reflect, journal or read. Still others identified a walkway, garden, or hiking trail. Each one had, consciously or not, designed a place for her spiritual life to be nourished.

Jesus is a primary model for prayer. The gospels describe his withdrawal from family, friends, and followers on a regular basis in order to retreat to the hills for quiet and solitude. In his instructions to his disciples he first points out the need to find a place to be alone. "Whenever you pray, go into your room and shut the door" (Matthew 6:6).

In the midst of bustling family routines, finding solitary space may seem next to impossible. With a lively combination of creativity and pragmatism, however, it can be done.

Furniture and Fixin's: Fashioning a Place of One's Own

Having a preferred place to sit during prayer has been part of my routine for many years. As our family moved from house to house over the years, this shifted from armchair to sofa and back again. Settling into this spot was a nonverbal signal to my husband and children that I had entered my sacred space and was not to be disturbed. On a nearby table I would light a candle and set out an object, such as a book or flower, which brought a sense of the holy to that spot. I rarely planned this out in great detail; it simply coincided with the flow of my life at the time.

It was only after doing this for a number of years that I realized I had created my own "domestic shrine." In doing this, I was following the example of various cultures and religious traditions that embrace the same custom in much more formal ways. The Japanese place small altars with a statue of Buddha in their homes. For the Navajo people, a hogan is believed to represent their universe in miniature. It is their most sacred space. Those growing up in Christian households might hang a cross on the wall or place a family Bible on a tabletop. The purpose in each instance is to draw us deeper into prayer and to remind us, in a concrete way, of the presence of the divine.

Circling: Tables and Other Places for Family Prayer

The most natural place for families to pray is undoubtedly around the table. It is here that we gather to eat meals, play games, and hold discussions. For some families, it may be the only place in which prayer occurs in a formal way.

When the house on Ivy Lane was being built, my mother insisted on enlarging the dimensions of the dining room. Her recognized need for a bigger room was both prophetic and purposeful. At the time she had only two children. Four more would arrive over the next several years, and spouses and grandchildren followed. Even though our dining room table could seat eighteen people when extended its full length, it eventually grew too small to accommodate everyone. This was the site of my first experience of communal prayer and ritual, and the impressions it made at a young age have stayed with me throughout my life. How grateful I am to my mother for her insight and wisdom.

The family table is a great place for children to learn to pray with others. Because it is such a natural environment to be together—eating, talking, and sharing stories—this learning comes quickly and at an early age.

Another common place for domestic prayer is the bedside. It offers a chance for parents to have one-on-one time with a child and is where many of us were taught specific prayers. Reading a story, chatting about one's day, asking God's blessing, settling under the blankets, and turning on a nightlight—all form a bedtime ritual that stays forever fixed in one's mind and heart.

Planes, Trains, and Automobiles: Prayer on the Run

Lord, keep your hand upon me as I travel and help me to reach my destination in safety.

This prayer, engraved on a magnet and stuck to the dashboard of our family car, was said routinely by my mother before she switched on the ignition. It became a custom that reminded us of our need for God's protective care. As highways become more hazardous, such reflection is more relevant than ever. It is also an example of how simply prayer can be used when on the road.

A few years ago, in a survey of preferences conducted among U.S. Catholics, the car was named the most favored place for prayer. This may have referred to nothing more than quickly muttered petitions in times of danger, but I suspect it runs deeper. As we spend greater amounts of time commuting to work, chauffeuring kids to school and soccer, running errands, and taking road trips, the car becomes a cocoon on wheels. It may be the only place in the course of a day where we are alone and free from other distractions.

A friend of mine claims that her favorite place to pray is the airport. Like the car, it provides an insular environment. While waiting for a flight to board, she pulls out her journal and writes. No one interrupts her and there are no work-related or household tasks she can, should, or wants to complete. This brief interlude serves as a transition as she moves from one town to the next. It provides breathing room that she doesn't find anywhere else.

Whether parents have a schedule that includes traveling to another country or just down the block, the possibilities for reflection while on the run are plentiful. This might entail turning off a cell phone and tuning in a CD of soothing music. It can mean focusing on one thing—driving, for example—and thus developing the spiritual discipline of attentiveness. Being out of the house can make us grateful for our surroundings, especially as we learn to slow down and watch for the beauty that otherwise lies unnoticed when we rush from one place to the next.

Dashboards no longer contain enough metal to hold a magnet, but contemporary families can still duplicate my mother's routine. The action of buckling a seatbelt and settling into place can be a trigger that reminds us to stop and ask for God's protection on our journey. In time, such activity becomes habit—a healthy and holy one that stays with us no matter where we are.

Sacred Sites: Family Pilgrimages and Explorations

A pilgrimage is a journey taken to a holy place in order to become closer to God. Some people take pilgrimages to the Holy Land or to a special church, shrine, temple, or mosque, for holy days or times of prayer. Over time people of all faiths have embarked on such journeys as a way to deepen their faith. The key to making a good pilgrimage is being open to how it might change and strengthen us by the time we return home. A pilgrimage does not have to be far away, however. There are many ways to take a journey to places we make holy by walking in the name of God.

When reminiscing about childhood, my daughter recalls our family hikes with fondness. These were often unplanned attempts to get out of the house when she and her brother were restless and out-of-sorts. I suppose being in the fresh air did us all good. On other occasions we went on outings that had a specific destination attached to them. While they might not qualify as pilgrimages, they did manage to bring us closer to one another and, I believe, to God.

Whether it is as elaborate as an excursion to a sacred place or as simple as a trip to a park, families can find spiritual enrichment in all sorts of places. Museums and zoos enable us to appreciate the gifts of history, nature, and science. Concerts and art galleries feed the spirit with beauty and creativity. Hiking trails and bike paths restore a sense of connection between physical exertion and spiritual fitness. Each has the potential to make us stronger by the time we return home.

In his book *Care of the Soul,* Thomas Moore places great emphasis on beauty's role in the well-being of the spirit. The time and attention given to artful architecture, he points out, affects the soul of the entire community. On the other hand, a stripping away of beauty due to crass planning, lack of funding, or a dearth of imagination, threatens our corporate spiritual health.

When one remains attentive, it is remarkable to notice how much beauty surrounds us. Along with being pilgrims, families also become explorers—seeking out "soulful" places in which to walk, ride, play, or pray, remaining ever alert to the hidden face of God within it all.

Creating Interior Space for Prayer

When Jesus described heaven, he never spoke of a place; rather he described a state of the heart. —Wayne Muller

Finding an external place to pray is a challenge. Creating internal space is an even greater one. This is especially true for parents whose many levels of responsibility at home, at work, and in the community keep them preoccupied and chronically overloaded.

There is a little statue on my desk called an inner manifestation bowl. It is a figure of a person seated in a cross-legged position. The shoulders and arms are extended out and down, and the fingertips are touching. This forms a small depression in the shape of a heart. It is meant to be a reminder of the daily need we have to seek and find the space within, the place of the inner heart.

The heart has played a role in most major religious traditions as a way to represent treasured beliefs, hopes, loves, and longings. "In the chronicle of our species, ever since we acquired speech and symbols, the imaginative place accorded to the heart can tell you a great deal about how a people defines itself and what it holds sacred" (Gail Godwin, *Heart*). The Bible makes reference to the heart as the site of spiritual growth and searching more frequently than it does the body, mind, or even the spirit.

In his book *The Inner Voice of Love,* Henri Nouwen, one of the greatest spiritual writers of the twentieth century, notes the need to seek the Wisdom within. Written during a turbulent period of his life, he speaks of the importance of daily retreat in prayer to a "place that is solid, the place where you can say yes to God's love even when you do not feel it." Only then can we find the most sacred part of ourselves—the inner heart. This is an essential piece of wisdom that is found in all spiritual traditions. While they may vary in approach, each includes something similar to these four components:

1. Slow Down
Speed is irrelevant if you're traveling in the wrong direction.

—Mahatma Gandhi

I once read a story about a mother with nine children, ranging in age from infancy to middle adolescence. In detailing how she managed meals, schedules, and mountains of laundry, she mentioned that she visited a retreat center near her home each day after dropping the older children at school. It was clear that this kept her sane.

Whether the exterior place for prayer is a hermitage or a house doesn't matter. What does is the interior slowing down and coming to a complete stop somewhere in the course of each day. Doing so situates us in a different kind of time by refocusing our attention and allowing us room to actually breathe.

As my children were growing, I found this stopping point shifting with the changing of their schedules. At first it occurred while they were napping. Then it came with the walks I took after Ron returned from work. When I took a job outside the home, it came as a twenty-minute respite in the morning before others were awake. I managed never to let go of it, no matter how hectic life seemed to get. Like the mother of nine children, I knew I had to stop at some point each day in order to preserve my peace of mind.

2. Be Quiet

Sacred space is soaking in deep silence.

I came across this quote years ago. It brings to mind the image of taking a long, luxurious bath, something most parents can only dream about after a long and stressful day.

All practices dealing with prayer and meditation stress the importance of being quiet, of listening, of stillness. At some point we need to escape from the external noise and withdraw as much as possible from distractions in order to enter a place of inner silence.

Shutting down the internal chatter is much more difficult. The clutter in our souls can parallel or outweigh that in our houses, leaving us drained and off-center. The "shoulds" and "oughts" of life may hound us, burdening us with guilt when we take time for our spiritual needs. The truth is that we cannot continue to function well if we are physically and spiritually exhausted. Soaking in silence is one way to replenish our drooping souls.

As mentioned earlier, my friend found that even an airport can be conducive to prayer. There was nothing she could do to shut down the surrounding sounds. When she began writing in her journal, however, the constant din turned into white noise. It reduced itself to a hum that she was able to disregard as she entered more intensely into internal space. The key for her lay in the journaling. It is an activity that draws her inward and provides a centering point. As words flow from the pen, her mind empties. This is an especially helpful quieting technique for extroverts who need to talk things out before they are ready to be still.

My friend's experience illustrates the endless possibilities of going with the flow of life. Rather than awaiting the perfect and most peaceful place to appear, we pray where we are. I have seen people sitting in stillness on park benches and subway seats. Backs erect and eyes closed, they are clearly not asleep, but in a state of meditation. If such locations are conducive to inner silence, the busiest household can be, too. Some additional techniques facilitate this kind of quiet and are easy to learn and implement.

One involves breathing—our most continual, natural, and largely unconscious activity. Thich Nhat Hanh, poet and Zen master, describes the breath as that which connects life to consciousness: "Whenever your mind becomes scattered, use your breath as the means to take hold of [it] again" (*Miracle of Mindfulness*). The process is straightforward: take in a deep breath and then breathe it all out again in a conscious act of exhalation. Concentrate all attention on this simple two-step process. When thoughts and "to-dos" crop up, clear them out again by pulling the mind back to breathing in and breathing out.

The calming effect of this simple practice is extraordinary. For parents, especially, it can be a way to soothe frazzled nerves, calm anxieties, and cope with large and small crises.

As one breathes in and out, the recitation of a phrase or one-word mantra also brings about a state of inner stillness. These might be the words "peace," "Jesus," or "Spirit," or phrases such as "God, be with me" or "Open my heart." Visualizing oneself in a favorite place, such as a beach or mountaintop, can also eliminate distractions and facilitate internal quiet.

3. De-Clutter

The inner heart is a place where we are truly at home. It is the locus of our deepest longings and our most intense desires. It is where God dwells in us.

Whenever I look at the inner manifestation bowl, I am struck by how compact the heart space is. It cannot hold much. Jesus often described the reign of God in small vs. grandiose images—mustard seeds, lost coins, and granules of yeast. He told his followers that the quest to find God was not in impressive edifices, elaborate rules, or the acquisition of power or riches. It would entail scaling back and letting go of all that is non-essential. Only then would we find the "pearl of great price" (Matthew 13:46).

His words resonate as powerfully today as they did two thousand years ago. Many of us carry around baggage, both external and internal, that needs to be jettisoned because it cannot fit into such a tiny heart space.

In the past several years, there have been a host of books written on the theme of simplicity. The trouble with many of them is that they are too complicated. By contrast, there is a three-step plan for simple living that works beautifully. I learned it several years ago from Sr. Jose Hobday, a gifted speaker and teacher. Simply stated, we need to take care of:

• all our needs

• some of our wants, and

• an occasional luxury.

In reality our deepest needs are minimal. It is why Jesus painted a verbal picture of free-flying birds and wildflowers when describing such needs, all of which are filled by a God who knows our hearts most fully. Identifying our wants and occasional luxuries is also critical because too much austerity can make us bitter and brittle.

A life based solely on needs may be one that is merely "functional," a condition Thomas Moore equates with loss of soul. By following a plan for simple living we learn, in time, to trust our inner voice. Such a process is one that Nouwen describes as "coming home" to a place that brings rest to our hearts.

4. Pay Attention

The account of Mary and Martha (Luke 10:39–42) is one that readily applies to modern households. Martha, busy with the details of preparing a meal for guests, is annoyed with her sister for not helping. Instead, Mary is sitting on the floor, listening to Jesus. In Martha's view she is shirking her responsibilities as a member of the family.

Some spiritual writers see this story as representative of the two sides of a single person caught between work and rest. Both are spiritual. Martha, however, gets hung up with a sense of duty that borders on martyrdom. It is not hard to imagine her growing resentment as she sets the table and stirs the stew. She has lost sight, Jesus reminds her, of the "greater part"—that of sitting still, of listening and learning, of opening the heart. The end result is a great deficiency in Martha's life. While her work is important, she has become distracted. Mary, on the other hand, remains attentive.

In *The Miracle of Mindfulness*, Thich Nhat Hanh uses the story of a young father with a hyperactive child to teach a lesson about attentiveness. The father appears to be in an impossible situation, one that raises an interesting question. How can a parent be mindful when there's so much to do?

Our culture honors "multi-tasking" as the ultimate in human ingenuity. This increases the pressure on parents to "do it all"—juggle child-rearing, household maintenance, marriage and relationships, jobs and careers, civic and religious involvement with precision and grace. Such a balancing act makes for an inordinate amount of distraction. More than a few balls come crashing down in the process.

Attentiveness, on the other hand, requires a bit of Mary-like behavior. Thich Nhat Hanh describes it as the essential discipline. It means being aware, from moment to moment, of where we are and what we are doing. When washing the dishes, we wash the dishes. The father in the story described a shift in his own busy life as he started to employ this practice. Rather than fracturing his time, being married and raising a young son gave him a sense of expansion. Once he became conscious of being present to those around him, he began to embrace a new sense of "unlimited" time. This is a hopeful insight for parents who feel panicked about the fleeting nature of their days.

Coming Home

Finding both external and internal spaces for prayer are not overnight endeavors. It takes time and discipline to make room in our lives and to retreat on a regular basis to those sacred places. When we do, it leads us to the inner heart, the "solid place" where we are most at home.

Guiding Your Child

Young children are great imitators. As author Robert Fulgham says, we shouldn't worry that they don't listen to us—we should worry that they are always watching us. When it comes to the "where" of prayer, nothing has a greater impact than modeling. When they witness their parents setting aside a place to "make holy," children soon learn to do the same. The important thing is to honor the space they, in turn, create for themselves. Children's questions about a parent's prayer space can also be an opportunity to discuss with them the value of solitude and quiet.

As children grow more independent, parents can help them seek their own places to pray. Identify spaces in the house and yard and talk to your child about where they can be away from the hub of family activity while still remaining safe. A small child might let other family members know she has entered her sacred space by sitting on a prayer rug in a corner or using a scarf or blanket on a couch or chair. Point out the value of distancing themselves from distractions, such as the television or computer, for short periods of time. Talk to them afterwards about how it felt to be in a place of one's own.

Older children start to withdraw naturally as they approach and enter adolescence. Parents need to respect their privacy and encourage healthy doses of solitude. At the same time, it is important to monitor a young person at this time to make sure she is not sinking into depression or swamped by loneliness. Providing inspirational books or magazines geared to teens or encouraging an interest in music or art can be a help. So, too, can sitting with a pet as a way to calm oneself and enter a period of quiet.

Families might initiate a ritual in which everyone retreats to his or her separate space for a set period of time. With young, hyperactive, or developmentally disabled children, or if this is a new experience, it is best to start small. Five minutes might be sufficient in the beginning. Gradually add a minute or two as everyone becomes comfortable with the routine. If a spouse is non-religious or uninterested in prayer, this activity can still be put to use without pressuring her or him to do anything other than enjoy a period of quiet. Few of us are going to object to that!

As children get older, out-of-the-house places for prayer become more abundant. This gives parents a chance to be together as a family or with a child on an individual basis. Visiting a monastery, retreat house, a different church or historic cemetery, walking a labyrinth, or taking a tour of an arboretum are all experiences that can broaden a young person's view of spirituality beyond what they may have dismissed as "boring."

Many of the ideas suggested for finding interior space for prayer can also be adapted for children. Resisting the urge to program each moment of a child's life goes against a mighty current in today's society. Far too many families are drowning in a sea of overcommitment. When children are small, give them free space in which to play quietly and by themselves. Incorporate a moment of silence into grace before meals and take a deep breath before starting the car. In time, these practices develop into patterns that children follow on their own.

Paring down possessions is something many families are happy to do. The need/want/luxury components of simple living are applicable to a child as well as to an adult. It is best, however, not to force the process; doing so creates resistance. Instead, aim for guiding children into discernment by asking questions and resurfacing memories. What, for example, have they found they really needed in the past day or week? How will this affect what they choose to do or acquire in the day(s) ahead? As they grow older, children will then become more adept in making the connections between external and internal clutter.

Our Family

Set aside time to take a walk through your home and assess the "where" of prayer in your family. Here are some questions to guide your discussion:

- Where are our favorite places to pray, by ourselves and as a family?
- What are some other places we could use for payer?
- What spaces and places make it hard to pray? Why? What can we do to make them holy space?
- What makes our house or apartment a home?
- What are some of our favorite "soulful" places?

Blessing Prayer for the Home

Blessed be all the rooms of this home.
May each of them be holy
and filled with the spirit of happiness.
> —Edward M. Hays, *Prayers for the Domestic Church*

CHAPTER 4

The Rhythm of Prayer

George Gershwin was a brilliant composer, renowned for his use of syncopated rhythm that placed emphasis on beats that are usually unaccented. In collaboration with his brother, Ira, he wrote a jazzy show tune called "Fascinating Rhythm" that makes liberal use of syncopation and celebrates the exuberance of rhythm that's "got me on the go."

Parenting includes lots of syncopated rhythm, benign moments that suddenly pulsate into something chaotic.

- The recognition that a suspected bout of "flu" is actually an unexpected pregnancy.
- The family vacation that takes a detour to an emergency room.

• The restful evening that morphs into pandemonium after a child confesses to "forgetting" about a science project due the next morning.

If one expects prayer to be undertaken only during times of quiet and calm, then family life is the last place to find it. The good news is that prayer is easily folded into the rhythm of our days, weeks, months, and years, no matter how offbeat these times are. Although it may not solve the problem of overstuffed schedules, prayer can help us shape the time we have been given.

Thomas Merton refers to the contemplative life as "compassionate time," providing us the space and grace in which to reflect upon how God is present to us in each moment. This happens not only during rare times of silence and solitude but also while we are on the go—dancing, sometimes wildly, to the fascinating rhythm of domestic life.

Daily Prayer

The different activities of our daily lives are not distractions from prayer but rather [its] rich soil. —Edward Hays

Praying throughout the day is a regular practice among Christians, Jews, and Muslims. The daily cycle, set in place by the rising and setting of the sun, contains particular "hours" for prayer. The bible refers to this in Psalm 119:164: "Seven times a day I praise you…" Early Christians marked these times of prayer at dawn (*prime* or first hour), nine AM (*terce* or third hour), noon (*sext* or sixth hour), three PM (*none* or ninth hour), six PM (*vespers* or evening hour) and night (*compline* or the hour of retiring). Over the centuries the Catholic Church compressed these into four—morning (*lauds*), noon, vespers, and compline.

Many of us long for someone to ring a bell, summoning us to periods of quiet and providing a break from the busyness that seems to be a given in modern life. Although not triggered by bell-tolling, there is nevertheless a rhythm to domestic life that contains natural stopping points throughout the day. We might call these the Liturgy of Family Hours.

Morning: Moving into Day

When my two children moved from cribs to beds, they experienced a new freedom that meant whenever they woke up they would get up. More than one morning was spent dragging myself to the kitchen to fix breakfast long before roosters thought to crow. My fervent prayer was that they would "sleep in" until at least six o'clock. Then I could face the day.

Then it shifted, seemingly overnight, to school-based routines. My daughter had been "blessed" with what Sr. Jose Hobday generously calls the "gift of leisure." Getting her up and ready was no small task. It is with a sense of amazement that I can look back at those days and recall sitting in my favorite chair and writing in my journal. This might have been due to being the first one up or else I was able to grab a few moments while everyone else was preoccupied. Having a helpful husband was a big factor, as was the growing ability of our children to get themselves dressed.

Being both a stay-at-home mother and, later, returning to the workplace brought both obstacles and opportunities. And, on the mornings when it was barely possible to eat a piece of toast before rushing out the door, I could still mutter a prayer asking for God's guidance and protective care over us all as the day began.

Morning is a time for such petition. We arise with a sense of anticipation or reluctance, depending upon the people we expect to encounter and the responsibilities we have to shoulder. Whenever possible, it helps to pause before bouncing out of bed. The prayer we offer at this time sets a positive and thoughtful rhythm for the hours that will follow.

Noontime: The Pause That Refreshes

The Gershwin brothers wrote another song that is my all-time favorite. "Summertime and the livin' is easy..." it begins. Hearing it reminds me of the summer lunches my mother laid out on our back porch—peanut butter sandwiches and potato chips, green grapes and pink lemonade, fresh strawberries and chocolate chip cookies. After eating, we lolled around the house, luxuriating in the laziness and freedom that the season encapsulated.

When I speak to young parents today, this is hardly the image that comes to their minds. "I dread summer," one mother told me as she listed the number of activities in which her children were involved. I guessed that the idea of siesta—in summer or winter— was out of the question for her.

Perhaps the back porch routine set by my mother is the reason I still love lunchtime. Being a morning person, I awaken early and put in several hours of work before the clock strikes twelve. As toddlers, my children tended to entertain themselves pretty happily during the morning hours, thus leaving me to pursue my own tasks and respon- sibilities. Then it was time to sit and eat and then to rest a while.

There seems to be an innate wisdom in napping after lunch. For those living in climates where the practice of siesta is routine, this is also practical. It is simply too hot to engage in anything else. Whether one is tending a child at home or working in an office, noontime provides a break that keeps the spirit spry and buoyant. We need a resting point halfway through the day in which to appre- ciate the bounty of God that is enfolded into our lives. Taking a stroll, savoring an apple, or lolling around the house are gateways to prayer that are rejuvenating and that move us through the rest of the day with greater ease.

Evening: From Rush Hour to Happy Hour

Another daily practice observed by my mother was taking a bath late in the afternoon. It formed part of a ritualistic holdover from another time and generation—that of resting and then changing clothes for dinner. To today's young mothers, the idea of a 4:00 PM bath is laughable. "Rush hour" not only refers to traffic jams and highway crawl; it is what occurs in thousands of home each day as parents and children return from work, school, or play. They are hungry, exhausted, and cranky enough to make the thought of locking oneself in the bathroom a tempting one.

Another old-fashioned evening hour practice, one associated with the "nifty fifties," is cocktail hour. It was grown-up time—a chance for parents, especially fathers, to let down after a hard day's work. In recent years, this practice has been repackaged as "happy hour" and resituated in bars and lounges.

For families, evening rituals of returning home, preparing for dinner, and settling around a table can be loaded with stress and strain. Gathering for a meal is becoming harder to achieve; recent surveys show that families do it an average of two times a week or less. Research also shows, however, that sharing a meal together is one factor in keeping families healthy. While the need to induce an hour of happiness through alcohol is rather dubious, there is merit to claiming this time for domestic strength, closeness, and joy.

As noted earlier, table time provides a setting for offering prayers of thanksgiving and blessing. When parents safeguard this time of day it becomes an hour that is shaped into something happy and holy.

Bedtime: Looking Back

I don't recall my father ever teaching me a prayer. He did, however, model a powerful way to pray when, at night, I would catch a glimpse of him kneeling by his bedside. An avid reader, he usually had a prayer book or pamphlet in hand. The memory of this strikes me as both humble and profound. After he died, we found numerous prayer cards, booklets, and readings tucked into the drawer of his nightstand. They revealed an even deeper side to his nightly routine.

While many parents make sure that their children say bedtime prayers, they may not be as vigilant about this practice themselves. Perhaps after a long day we are too tired to get on our knees, literally or figuratively. The benefits to such prayer are so plenteous, however, that, once discovered, we rarely want to miss them. Bedtime is opportune for running through the day's events and reflecting upon them.

One of my favorite practices involves taking a spiritual inventory of the way I was made aware of God through use of my senses. I call it the FSSST prayer—one in which I count off on the fingers of one hand what physical feelings, sounds, sights, smells, and tastes were part of my day. Such an exercise fosters a greater awareness of the sensate experience of the Divine Mystery that surrounds us if we take time to notice.

Examining one's conscience is another bedtime practice that assesses how well we spoke or acted towards others in the course of the day. Rather than providing us with a reason to feel guilty or ashamed, such an exercise helps us view our behavior with honesty, humility, and a dose of humor. We can then make a mental effort to end the day by unloading all of our burdens, entrusting them to God so that we can get a good night's sleep.

Midnight: Insight and Anxieties

My friend Sue once gave me a rosary made by her grandmother. In an accompanying note, she explained that its mismatched blue beads were meant to signify the unevenness of life experience. Her grandmother, she said, would often hold the rosary rather than say it. The practice allowed her to loosen her grip on fear and anxiety and surrender everything to God.

I cherish this rosary and keep it beside my bed. More than once

I have reached for it during the night, a time when I often use prayers of intercession. When agonizing over a baby's fever, an adolescent's rebellion, or a ballooning mortgage payment, we can turn to the saints as well as to deceased parents and grandparents, leaning on their ability to pray for us when our worries become too much to handle.

Nighttime prayer isn't all about anxiety, however. Great insights come when we lie awake in the dark, surrounded by peace and calm. The mind in such a state of rest is able to sort out in the middle of the night what kept it stymied during the day. Quiet conversation with a wakeful spouse can be prayer-full in its intimacy, providing uninterrupted space to share hopes and dreams. Such time allows us to name and claim the blessings in our lives and to see each one with greater clarity under the light of a thousand stars.

Seasonal Prayer

I love calendars. They appeal to intuitive types like me, those who revel in making plans and imagining the future. The calendars in my home are plentiful—they hang on the kitchen wall, sit on my desk, and rest in my purse. Every Christmas, my husband and children can count on receiving their favorite type of calendar from me, one thematically woven with their current interest in art, literature, or humor.

As commonplace as calendars are today, it was not always so. At one time, the practice of looking into the future and counting days, weeks, and seasons was considered too sacred for ordinary folks to pursue. Thus, calendars were reserved for priests and shamans—those deemed holy enough to make wise use of their powers.

Whether one considers calendar-keeping a joy or a pain, there is no question that family life is lived out amongst the rituals and routines of the weeks, months, and seasons that constitute a year.

Holidays and holydays, family events and weekly cycles all provide an ongoing context for prayer that enables us to embrace the past, savor the present, and anticipate the future.

The Weekly Cycle

Bundled into a seven-day cycle, each week contains a rhythm that plays out as the days progress. Sunday is a day Christians set aside for worship and rest. Based on the Jewish Sabbath, "it is to be holy, a time intentionally set apart from ordinary work and family tasks to allow for maintenance, renewal, and the soul's progress" (Robert C. Morris, "Soul Time," in *Weavings*, vol. XIV). Unfortunately for many of us, the meaning of the day has been overtaken by household chores, shopping, and others types of work and activity.

As my children were growing up, we often took advantage of Sunday's Sabbath symbolism by going to church and then embarking on a family outing, such as a hike, or visiting a park or zoo. Being away from house and phone (those were pre-wireless days) opened up a bit of breathing room to be more aware of God's splendor and grace. I consider these the sweetest of times, ones capped off with a Sunday dinner in the dining room or at a local pizza parlor. Such "soul time" is necessary for the maintenance of domestic as well as individual spirituality. Whether it's tossing a ball around in the backyard or sharing an elaborate meal, the reclaiming of Sunday as a time of worship and rest is a vital way for families to build a spiritual life that renews itself on a weekly basis.

Routines settle back into place as the weekdays take hold. In families of old, each day had its particular tasks—washing, ironing, baking, and mending—that took up an entire day. Thanks to modern appliances we can accomplish these things in a simultaneous fashion while also leaving home for jobs and school. With all of these "conveniences," however, contemporary life can be hectic as the weekday calendar fills in with meetings, appointments, and commitments. Punctuating each day with moments of prayer, through a Liturgy of Family Hours, helps maintain a domestic spirituality in the midst of busy weeks.

As a child, I reveled in the freedom that Saturdays represented, especially when my brother and I arose at dawn for a morning of watching cartoons. While this final day of the week is often given over to chores, errands, and soccer matches, there is a playful aspect to it that families might harness as part of their spiritual routine. "Prayers on the go" are especially appropriate and the recalling of blessings received is a fitting way to bring closure to the seven-day cycle.

Holidays: The Power of Ritual and Tradition

Picture a European peasant living in the Middle Ages. It brings to mind a hand-to-mouth existence, one characterized by sunrise-to-sunset toil. It comes as a surprise, then, to discover that this same peasant, by some estimates, had one third of the year "off" to celebrate holidays and seasons. Tied to the earth's cycles and clocked to the natural light provided by the sun, this same peasant did not put in as many working hours as the average American today.

There was much to celebrate and observe—the spring equinox that increased the temperature and number of daylight hours, the fertile cycles of crops and livestock, the births and deaths of royal figures, and the lives of revered saints and heroes. Each holiday came with its particular set of rituals and traditions, generally tied to the enjoyment of food and drink. Such practice taught by doing and uncovers one of the most fundamental ways to pray within the home and faith community.

The calendar year contains a number of secular holidays. Some of these are established in a formal way and observed as such. American Thanksgiving, for example, was named a federal holiday by Congress in 1942 and set on the fourth Thursday of November. Its roots extend deep into American soil, back to the founding of the Plymouth colony and the three-day festival celebrated by pilgrims and Native Americans. The sharing of foods such as turkey, cranberries, and yams link the holiday with its earlier origins—the marking of harvest with feasting and festivity. Overlaying it today are cultural traditions made possible by modern technology (televised football games) and individual family customs that pass from one generation to the next.

In many homes, the celebration of holidays is undertaken with great care and attention to detail. Out come the "tools" for such observations—the good china for Thanksgiving, and red, white, and blue paper plates for the Fourth of July. We bake or barbeque according to custom, and dress up or down to create the environment and mood appropriate to the season.

None of this is ever explained to us, of course. We learn what various holidays mean by participating with parents and grandparents, siblings, cousins, and friends in the preparation, sharing, and later recollection of each one. Repeating these celebrations with the turning of each year's cycle further reinforces our knowledge, appreciation, and recognition of the rituals, symbols, and stories that accompany each one. While we may not make a conscious connection with the peasant of long ago, we relate at some level to his experience through the way in which we ritualize our own celebration of special days and times.

A ritual is defined as a patterned way of doing something, one that is honed through repetition. We learn the pattern of celebrating Halloween by dressing up, carving pumpkins, and trick-or-treating, and by doing these things over again each year. We use symbols that become familiar through consistent use and associations with particular days and seasons. Thus we are not likely to see people fixing eggnog on July 4 or placing jack-o-lanterns in their windows on Easter. Such repetition creates a sense of identity within our family, ethnic group, church, or society. It also provides stability and offers comfort during times of grief or trauma. "Getting back to normal" often means that we can celebrate the way we used to with familiar rituals, symbols, and traditions.

The use of rituals is an important way that families pray together. Through them we express our spiritual and religious values. We give thanks, acknowledge our need for one another, and celebrate our blessings. In their book, *Rituals for Home and Parish*, Jack Rathschmidt and Gaynell Bordes Cronin describe the link between domestic traditions and those that take place at church. Home ritual, they state, is what makes Sunday worship all the more meaningful because it contains symbols that have a power greater than themselves. Such symbols "put us in touch with meaning and mystery in a way nothing else can."

Thus, the dramatic flair with which my father carved and dished out the turkey each Thanksgiving brings to mind his powerful role as patriarch and provider in our family. Around the table, year after year, our extended family relived an ancient and artful tradition of giving thanks for the bountiful harvest that was placed before us.

Holydays: Cycling With the Liturgical Year

"Do we have to go to Mass this year? I've heard that story before." When my son posed this question at the age of ten, hoping to bypass church that Christmas, he unwittingly made some good observations about the liturgical year—namely that it is both cyclic and repetitive. When the feast of Christmas draws round again we do indeed hear the same story. We also use the same rituals, symbols, and songs to celebrate our belief in Christ's coming.

While most secular calendars are linear, the liturgical year is usually depicted in circular form. Sacred seasons are marked off and shaded with their corresponding liturgical colors—green, red, white, and purple. Each one contains particular feasts and celebrates a different aspect of the Christian story. Even though modern culture has secularized some of these holydays with symbols such as Santa Claus and the Easter Bunny, their powerful religious meanings remain strong if we take care to notice them.

Thus, the celebration of the church year is a beautiful way for families to express their faith. And, while hearing the same stories over and over again may seem redundant, each one takes on deeper relevance as we hear it anew each time around. Taking a brief walk around the church year reveals connections to family life that makes its stories and symbols rich with meaning and purpose.

• *The liturgical year begins with Advent, the four weeks (counted by Sundays) prior to Christmas.* This is a season of preparation, waiting, and anticipation. We ready ourselves to celebrate the coming of Jesus in two ways—by recalling his historical birth over 2000 years ago and by looking ahead to his second coming at the end of the world. The readings from the lectionary, the sequence of readings used at Sunday Mass and throughout the week, reflect these themes as prophets and angels foretell what is to come.

Coinciding in the northern hemisphere with the winter solstice, the season also marks the movement out of darkness and into the lengthening days that will continue until summer. The lighting of Advent wreaths, in both churches and homes, marks the four weeks of the season by growing increasingly brighter as the promise of Christmas approaches. The color of the season is purple (blue-violet)—a symbol of royalty.

At this time of year families are caught up with Christmas customs and cherished traditions. There are foods to prepare and visitors to welcome, gifts to give and to receive, decorations to be hung and parties to attend. For some, this is a season of stress as expectations and responsibilities increase in intensity. When the commercial aspects of Christmas overshadow its original intent, it is important for families to choose how and where they will spend their time, money, and energy. Reflecting upon the humble circumstances surrounding the birth of Jesus can refocus the season into something quiet, simple, and filled with peace.

• *In the church year, Christmas is both a holyday and a season.* The latter extends from the eve of Christmas to the feast of the Baptism of Jesus in mid-January. Several feast days that celebrate the life of Jesus are situated in this season—the Holy Family, Mary, the Mother of God, and the Epiphany, to name a few. The color shifts to white, which signifies joy, purity, and victory.

As a new calendar year is rung in, families can name their hopes that coincide with the church's celebration of this God-in-our-midst season. Keeping Christmas decorations in place, at least until the feast of the Epiphany (January 6), helps extend the meaning of Christmas beyond that of a single day and into an entire season.

• *Lent is the forty-day preparation period prior to Easter.* Even though the prelude to the season occurs on Ash Wednesday, the forty-day countdown doesn't begin until the first Sunday in Lent. It continues until the evening of Holy Thursday. Three traditional practices are emphasized during this season—prayer, penance, and almsgiving. Originally it was set aside as a time of preparation for those who were to be baptized on Easter. Lent is a time of spiritual spring cleaning through intensifying our prayer life, fasting from food or bad habits, and performing acts of charity and justice. The color of the season is purple (red-violet) symbolizing penitence, passion, and suffering.

Lenten simplicity holds great potential for families who feel stressed by the accumulation of unnecessary stuff crowding their homes. These forty days provide an impetus for cleaning out closets and giving away clothes and household items to those who can make better use of them. Fasting and abstaining take on enriched meaning when one "gives up" such domestic habits as bickering over trivial matters or watching too much television and striving to be more loving and attentive to one another. Parishes often sponsor projects that provide money or time to persons in need. And praying simple lenten devotions before or after meals is an additional way for families to deepen their commitment to faith.

• *The high point of the church year comes with the celebration of the Paschal Triduum*—the "three days" that commemorate the life, death, and resurrection of Christ. They begin with the celebration of the Lord's Supper on Holy Thursday and continue with the reading of the Passion and veneration of the cross on Good Friday. The Easter Vigil is celebrated on the night of Holy Saturday and includes a number of beautiful rituals, such as the lighting of the Easter fire and Paschal candle. Easter Sunday dawns with the celebration of the Eucharist and the joyful sounds of alleluias over the good news of Christ's resurrection from the dead. The colors of the Triduum are white for Holy Thursday and Easter, and red, symbolic of fire and blood, on Good Friday.

One of the rituals enacted on Holy Thursday is the washing of the feet, a gesture Jesus performed in the gospel of John (chapter 13) to show his disciples how they must serve one another. Such action is pervasive in the life of parents as they bathe, bandage, and blanket their children in love. The celebration of the Triduum contains powerful stories and symbols of dying and rising to new life. This, too, is part of a family's experience whenever they dive into and emerge from grief, loss, disillusionment, and disappointment. The coloring of eggs, donning of new clothes, and planting of gardens all have deep spiritual roots in Easter's hope and promise.

• *Like Christmas, Easter is both a holyday and a season.* The latter extends for fifty days and culminates with the feast of Pentecost, the traditional "birthday" of the church. While Lent is a season for fasting, Easter is one of feasting as we revel in the greening of the earth and the emergence of new life. Stories of Jesus' appearances to his disciples and his ascension into heaven are heard in the liturgies at this time of year. Each is filled with expectation and wonder as we await his coming again in full glory. The colors for this season are white and red (Pentecost).

The American school year comes to a close in most communities by the middle of June. Graduations mark the ending of one phase of life and the commencement of another. May is traditionally dedicated to Mary and therefore a fitting month to celebrate Mother's Day. The latter was originally proposed as an international day of peace, an appropriate theme for family prayer. The coming of the Holy Spirit to the disciples on Pentecost is a reminder of the strengthening of heart and soul that we each need in order to live faith-full lives.

• *There are two periods during the church year called Ordinary Time.* The first occurs in the brief interlude between the end of the Christmas season and the beginning of Lent. The second is much longer, extending from the end of the Easter season to the last Sunday of the liturgical year, the feast of Christ the King.

The term "ordinary" does not mean these are plain or uneventful seasons. Rather, it is derived from the word "ordinal," which means to count. Until recently in the Catholic Church these seasons were counted as Sundays after Epiphany and Pentecost, a practice still observed by Anglicans, Lutherans, and others. During this time we continue to celebrate the life of Jesus and the faith and dedication of his disciples. The lectionary contains stories of Jesus' ministry, calling us to imitate him as we go about our everyday lives.

The "ordinary time" in family life is a week-to-week process as well, one in which we change and grow. By counting off the weeks and months on family calendars, we can be mindful of how God is present to us each day and the ways in which we can respond with love, mercy, and compassion.

The Family Calendar

In addition to holidays and sacred seasons families live through their own particular cycles, ones marked by daily routines and points of transition. Each is an opportunity to recognize God's presence through the humdrum moments that accumulate into a lifetime.

Transition Points

Domestic life is made up of a series of beginnings and endings. We are born, take our first step, start school, learn to drive, date, graduate, get a job, marry or remain single, have children and then grandchildren. We experience the death of a parent, spouse, or child, outgrow clothes, toys, and relationships, divorce or separate, lose our job, health, or our dreams. We move to a new town or change careers.

In each instance there is a dying to an old way of life and a birthing to the new. Each transition is a sacramental moment, one in which signs of God's presence are made manifest through the ordinary experiences of life. This, in turn, opens up possibilities for giving expression to prayer in its various forms.

- New beginnings are times for prayers of praise, blessing, thanksgiving, and adoration.

- Rites of passage draw out of us petitions for the well-being and safety of our children and ourselves.

- Deaths and losses extract cries from deep inside of us as we struggle to forgive, to let go, to grieve, and to move on.

As one year grows into the second and eventually into a decade, prayer helps families to face, accept, and embrace the changes that make up the rhythm of hours, days, weeks, and years.

Guiding Your Child

Children start learning about ritual and tradition as soon as they join the family for meals. Although we don't take much notice of it, the transition from high chair to table is significant because of the expectations that accompany it. We anticipate that a child will start to take part in family discussions, learn table manners, and assist with meal preparation and clean-up. All of this develops gradually, to be sure, but is a vital process in which children become initiated into the rhythm of family life.

As children grow, their understanding of and participation in sacred and seasonal celebrations increases. They learn by doing. Storytelling constitutes a natural part of this process as we offer explanations and anecdotes about family rituals and traditions, and share memories and associations about symbols and actions. This can then lead to the drawing out of religious meaning and spiritual themes. Simple connections can be made, for example, between a family's coloring of Easter eggs and the significance of the egg as a symbol of the new life of Christ's resurrection.

Using blessings to mark special points in the growth and development of a child increases awareness of God's love and caring presence. This includes everything from losing a baby tooth to graduating from high school. Weaving prayer into daily routines and weekly schedules is another way to make it a continual practice. And using seasonal prayers and practices, such as lighting an Advent wreath or making the Stations of the Cross during Lent, provides a dynamic way to mark the turning of the liturgical seasons.

There comes a time in many families when children, perhaps as they approach and enter adolescence, roll their eyes at traditions and denounce them as boring or irrelevant. This may be an indication that they have outgrown rituals that are more appropriate for young children. More often, however, parents need to hold firm in maintaining traditions even when children balk at them. Once reaching a certain age or stage of life, children often return to those traditions, seeking and recognizing in them a stabilizing force in their lives.

Our Family

• Read over the Liturgy of Family Hours which begins on p. 47. How does your family, together or individually, make prayer a part of your daily routine? In what ways would you like to make this more intentional? How will you go about doing this?

• Using your family calendar, walk through the upcoming year together. As you go, ask each person to mark his or her favorite holydays, holidays, and seasons. Identify foods, customs, and stories that accompany them. Where and how did your family traditions start? How have they changed over the years?

In the Evening

O Lord, support us all the day long, until the shadows lengthen, and the evening comes, and the busy world is hushed, and the fever of life is over, and our work is done. Then in thy mercy, grant us a safe lodging, and a holy rest, and peace at the last. Amen.

—The Book of Common Prayer, 63

CHAPTER 5

When It's Hard to Pray

Pray in the Spirit at all times in every prayer and supplication.
—Ephesians 6:18

Paul's advice to the Ephesians seems simple enough. What happens when we can't pray? Or when our prayer is less a "surge of the heart" and more an act of sheer will, one that feels dry, forced, and confused? The truth is that, at some point, each of us will experience periods of distraction, dryness, and dread. Rather than giving up, we can face these times with resilience and determination and eventually find grace in them. Common challenges for parents and families are finding space for prayer in the busy pace of life, and facing grief and loss, trouble and stress. Here are some thoughts on each and how we can pray our way through the hard times.

Battling Busyness and Distraction

When speaking to groups of parents I ask what challenges they face. The response is always the same: too much to do and too little time. We are a busy society. Parents are stretched thin with jobs to maintain, households to manage, and children to care for. Add kids' activities, school involvement, and obligations at church and in the community and there is little free time left—for prayer or anything else.

Even when we do set aside the time, we may find ourselves battling distraction as the things we "should" be doing start to creep into our thoughts and trouble our hearts. Unable to concentrate, we give up and take off in a mad dash to catch up with all that can never be accomplished in a single day. In time, the prayer we do manage to offer seems dry and lifeless, as if we are only going through the motions in order to tick another to-do off the list.

Martin Luther King, Jr., once observed that if our day is busy, we should pray more. It is advice worth heeding. Those times of life that are crammed full of appointments and obligations are ones most in need of prayer. The precious five minutes we claim in the morning can make the whole day less frantic. I often find, when I awaken in a panic over all that has to be done in the day ahead, that sitting still for a few minutes, day-planner in hand, helps me to quiet down and think more clearly.

Just as sediment settles to the bottom when turbulent waters are allowed to become still, so can our busy demands take on greater clarity when we prioritize them in prayer. This entails letting go of all that we cannot, should not, or dare not control. By giving our day over to God we find a resting point that will remain fixed deep within ourselves, providing direction and balance as we work our way through each responsibility, task, and commitment.

Battling distraction is another challenge. In chapter three, we looked at the external and internal clutter that creates distraction. Turning off telephones and TVs and "rewiring" the atmosphere through the use of soothing music or the sound of a small water fountain can reduce or eliminate external noise. Internal clutter can be managed through centering exercises, mantras, journaling, and other methods that quiet a case of "monkey mind." A change of environment can also help. When we are nervous or anxious, taking a walk releases excess energy and restores a sense of calm. Reading a passage from Scripture or a book of reflections can re-channel our thoughts away from what's distracting us and onto a fresh spiritual path.

Dealing with distraction can be fairly simple when it is a matter of getting settled enough to pray. There are times, however, when our spiritual malady runs deeper. We may feel a dryness in our prayer that leaves us flat, uninterested, or just plain bored. There is a word for this state of the soul—acedia. It is generally defined as laziness or lax practice and a lack of vigilance in prayer, something that can easily happen in the crunch of busy schedules. I prefer the definition that Catherine of Sienna applied to acedia, that of spiritual depression. It occurs as a result of exhaustion, worry, and feeling overwhelmed, realities that parents know all too well.

As with mild mental depression, there are ways to deal with acedia that help to manage and eventually extract us from it. We know, for example, that physical exercise, laughter and certain foods release endorphins, feel-good hormones, into the brain that help alleviate depression. In similar fashion, there are ways to find and utilize "spiritual endorphins" that counteract the effects of acedia. The gratitude journal mentioned in chapter two is an example of one that I personally found to pull me out of a slump.

Thomas Moore notes that a serious indication of "loss of soul" is when life becomes all function—a "have-to" approach to living. The antidote, he says, lies in seeking out beauty. Listening to music, visiting an art gallery, or simply studying the design of a leaf each comprises an appreciation exercise that sets the soul back on course. This is not an instantaneous "fix" to acedia, but one that eventually helps us reclaim prayer as a cherished practice when we are depleted, distracted, or depressed.

Dealing with Grief and Loss

Tears are the prayer-beads of all of us… because they arise from a fullness of the heart. —Edward Hays

When Jenny died, Ron and I knew a grief as wide and deep as anything we could have ever imagined. I can still see us, standing in a hospital corridor, clinging to each other in sorrow and pain. It felt as if we were utterly alone and that no one could come close to understanding the depth of our loss.

"Tears," writes Edward Hays in *Pray All Ways,* "are an expression of lack of control. They are prayer because prayer is communion with that which is beyond our control: God." There may be nothing that feels as beyond our control as the death of a child. Everything about it is out of sync. Parents should outlive their children. We should also be able to safeguard them from danger and dying. And yet we can't. In the end, we are not in control—of their lives or even our own. It is a frightening reality that may break us in two with grief or consume us with bitterness and anger. The "prayer-beads" of tears, however, also contain an unexpected treasure—that of being able to let go and entrust our lives, and those of our children, to God.

We cannot protect ourselves from loss. It is part of the human experience, be it the death of a loved one, the erosion of health, or the devastation of divorce. The way we deal with it, and eventually heal, is through grieving. Over the centuries humans have devised a number of rituals that take us through the mourning process. Such rituals enable us to move through and past stages of denial and anger and into ones of acceptance and healing. Over time they restore a sense of peace, even if the hole left in our lives is never completely filled in again.

Woody Allen once observed that Americans seem to consider death as optional. Perhaps our technological advances and scientific breakthroughs, as stunning as they are, have given us the illusion that we can live forever. Whatever the reason, there is huge denial taking place in our culture about death and loss. It makes grieving hard to do.

Another part of this difficulty, ironically enough, is the rise in support groups. On the one hand, these have been a tremendous help in enabling people to step out of their loneliness and isolation by talking to those who have had similar experiences. On the other hand, we are expected to take our grief to meetings at a scheduled day and time, and to otherwise "get on" with life as quickly as possible. For the bereaved, however, there is no fixed time for dealing with such losses. They have to walk through them and are often expected to do it in a way that won't make anyone else uncomfortable.

At such times prayer can either flow freely out of the depth of our pain or remain stilted and stifled due to anger or depression. In her book, *Praying Our Goodbyes*, Joyce Rupp explains the value of prayer in the process of grieving. "When we pray a goodbye we do more than just pray about loss....We enter into the whole matter; we live it." According to Rupp, rather than increasing our sadness or creating an obsession with our loss, prayer enables us to recognize and reflect upon it, to use rituals that promote healing, and to reorient ourselves by bringing "faith to our grief." Praying our way through loss is a transformative process, one that enables us to recognize God's work in even the most distressing aspects of our lives.

It has been over twenty-five years since Ron and I held each other in that hospital hallway. Since then I have been able to see that we were not alone on that day. God was there, too, weeping along with us and beckoning us more fully into the great mystery of death and what lies beyond it.

Keeping the Faith in Times of Trouble

Faith is willing to engage the unknown, not shrink back from it.

—Shawn Salzberg

The summer of 2002 was a nerve-wracking one for parents. A string of kidnappings, including that of Elizabeth Smart, set the nation on edge and heightened concerns about the safety of our children. As news of one of the abductions was breaking, I received a phone call from a young mother in my parish. She explained how traumatized she was by these events and how much she feared for her six-year-old daughter. She was also struggling with her faith, angry that God could allow such things to happen. It left her unable to pray and in a state of agitation and despair. What, she asked, could she do?

There is no shortage of news accounts and imagined scenarios to stir parents' fears. Likewise, there are innumerable forms of trouble and stress that can strain our ability to pray. Sometimes, like this young mother, we are filled with outrage at God's seeming absence and indifference. Other times, our own angers, resentments, and unresolved issues, ones that constrain our ability to pray in any form that seems genuine, stymie us. In the face of such difficulty, it is a struggle to keep the faith. We can pray through such troubled states of the heart by embracing both hope and forgiveness.

The Prayer of Hope

For surely I know the plans I have for you, says the Lord, plans for your welfare and not for harm, to give you a future with hope. Then when you call upon me and come and pray to me, I will hear you. When you search for me, you will find me. —Jeremiah 29:11–13

The best encouragement I could offer the young mother was in and through hope. While the likelihood of something horrible happening to her daughter was slim, we both knew there were no guarantees. It is what makes parenting a terrifying task. Hope is a powerful means to confronting our fear, however. It anchors us in a trust that, no matter what might befall us, God does have a future in mind for us.

In reference to its position as one of the three theological virtues, hope has been described as both a middle child and a little girl, caught between and overshadowed by her two "bigger sisters"—faith and love. We certainly don't focus the attention on it that we do the other two virtues. Indeed, we sometimes wrongly confuse hope with either optimism—seeing silver linings in every dark cloud—or wishful thinking. When pulled out as a last resort ("There's nothing to do now but hope"), we equate it with hopelessness.

Hope is none of these things. "It is rather the certainty that something makes sense, is worth the cost, regardless of how it may turn out" (Michael Downey, "Gift's Constant Coming," in *Weavings*, vol. XIV). One of the most powerful expressions of hope occurs in the deceptively simple prayer of Julian of Norwich, a fourteenth century mystic: "All shall be well and all shall be well and all manner of things shall be well."

The Bible contains plenty of examples of those who, like the young mother, vented their frustration at God. Such rage is a form of cursing, a word that at its root means to restrain and bind and leads to a diminishment of the spirit. Job curses the day he was born (Job 3:3) and the prophet Jeremiah, after being beaten and imprisoned, accuses God of deceiving him and berates himself for falling prey to such deception. "O Lord, you have enticed me, and I was enticed; you have overpowered me, and you have prevailed. I have become a laughingstock all day long; everyone mocks me" (Jeremiah 20:7).

Job later comes to realize how little he knows of God's ways and Jeremiah speaks of not being able to contain the word of God because it burns so powerfully within him. Both go on to offer words of blessing, the opposite of cursing. They move from a stance of clenched fists to one of open hands. As a physical gesture, releasing the tension that accompanies a clenched fist is one that brings relief and freedom. It symbolizes the power of prayer offered in hope. We may not receive an instant answer to our supplications or find a happy ending to tragic occurrences. But we are, in time, able to bless God for what we cannot yet see or know and to rest in the hope that, in the end, "all shall be well."

The Prayer of Forgiveness

Let us shut the door on the past—not in order to forget it but in order not to allow it to imprison us. —Archbishop Desmond Tutu

In a conversation with another mother, I learned a great lesson about the meaning of forgiveness. This woman had recently been divorced and was struggling to let go of the anger and resentment she held against her ex-husband. "I want to let go of the power he has to keep hurting me and my children." In a nutshell, she summed up the benefits of forgiveness and the potential it has to liberate us from a past that can keep us imprisoned by our own resentment, guilt, hurt, anger, or fear.

In the Lord's Prayer forgiveness refers to a process that both seeks it and extends it to others. "And forgive us our trespasses, as we forgive those who trespass against us." Nowhere is this more critical than in the home where the splintering of relationships can be so destructive.

The most famous of Jesus' parables about forgiveness takes place within the context of the family. Known as "The Prodigal Son" (Luke 15:11–32) it is a timeless tale about the devastating effects of broken relationships and long-held resentments. While the story ends happily for the runaway son—his father welcomes him home with a party—we are left to guess about the fate of the older brother. Filled with indignity and more than a touch of self-inflicted martyrdom at being the "faithful" son, he refuses to join in the festivities for his brother. His father meets him, too, on the road and urges him to come inside, but we never learn whether he complies.

Be it in a pigsty or a prison, it is torturous to remain alienated from those we love. Praying to be forgiven and to be capable of forgiving others is an empowering step forward. "When we pray to be able to forgive, we are praying to be made larger…" (Muller). Such internal spaciousness enables us to bear the hurts without letting them snap us in two. Their power over us gradually diminishes and is replaced by the gracious love, mercy, and kindness of God.

Guiding Your Child

Running into dry spots and troubled situations is hard enough for us as parents. Handling restlessness and resistance towards prayer from our children can be exhausting, demoralizing, and disheartening. It often feels easier to give up.

Little children have limited attention spans, so holding their focus for even short prayers can be difficult. Eliminating physical distraction through some of the techniques described in this and previous chapters will help. So, too, will consistency. Through it children learn the discipline required to be still and to listen as well as to speak.

As children get older, their complaints about family prayer being boring or irrelevant can be countered by a reminder that prayer doesn't always feel good or exciting. It has been said that the only one who prays well is the one who prays often. Therefore, maintaining a regular pattern of prayer, even if it shifts as children go through various stages, is vital.

Children carry their own particular share of worries, fears, and sadness. Prayer can be a helpful way for them to give expression to these. As they approach adolescence, children are often reticent to speak about such concerns, especially to parents. Encouraging them to take their troubles to God through journaling, reflection, and meditation can bring a feeling of release and relief. Be careful not to promise ready-made answers and talk, if you can, about the mystery of God that is beyond our knowing. Prayer, as we have noted, isn't always comforting nor does it always come easily. And, it may be that God is directing us to seek help from others, in the form of spiritual direction or counseling, when our worries become too much to bear.

Helping children grieve their losses, both large and small, will serve them well throughout their lives. Joyce Rupp's four steps in saying good-bye is a simple yet beneficial process to use with even small children. Recognizing a loss means naming it and what it has meant. The death of a pet dog, for example, brings about feelings of sadness, perhaps accompanied by anger or remorse if an accident was involved. Reflecting upon it helps to surface the repercussions of such a loss. The dog is no longer there to protect the family, which makes for feelings of fear or insecurity. Or the dog's absence at the foot of a bed or on family outings can bring about a sense of loneliness and longing.

Rituals, such as a burial or telling stories, bring comfort and closure. Reorienting ourselves to life without a pet might raise questions about acquiring another one or being thankful for the memory of the dog and its place within the family. Throughout the grieving process, prayer can be folded into each step, bringing comfort and eventual healing.

Simple prayers of forgiveness can be introduced early in a child's life and become more complex as they grow. The parable of the prodigal son can be read and discussed together as a way to describe the process that forgiveness entails. This includes recognizing and confessing the way we have hurt and been hurt by others as well as asking for and extending forgiveness. Depending on the depth of one's pain and magnitude of the break in relationship, this might take a long time. Once again, marking each step with prayer grounds it in the hope we have in God's mercy and the power that is manifest in being set free from the past.

Our Family

Here are some questions to discuss together.

- When has prayer come hard for us as a family?
- What have we done in the past to break through it?

Plea for Deliverance from Suffering and Hostility

My God, my God, why have you forsaken me?
Why are you so far from helping me,
  from the words of my groaning?
O my God, I cry by day, but you do not answer;
And by night, but find no rest.

—Psalm 22:1–2

CHAPTER 6

Staying Spiritually Fit

My husband is a mountain runner. Five years ago, after being sidelined by a knee injury he set his heart on completing the Pikes Peak Marathon and placing in his age group. He devised a rigorous training schedule in order to prepare himself for the daunting run up and down the 14,000-foot peak.

Observing his training process has been fascinating. As Ron explained various aspects of the discipline and practices required, I began to appreciate the similarities between meeting such a physical challenge and the maintenance of a spiritually vigorous life. Playing off of these, I have identified five lessons I have learned from him about keeping spiritually fit.

Begin with the Small Steps

A knee injury kept Ron from running for over five years. Thus, when he began to train for the marathon, he had to proceed carefully. This excruciatingly slow process entailed running for one minute and walking for one, for a total of fifteen minutes to start. He increased this ratio slightly until he had worked his way to training runs of up to four hours. It took him three years to get to that point.

I have known people who, in their fervor to jumpstart a prayer routine, have taken on more than they could handle. Burnout and discouragement are usually the end results. It is not realistic, for example, to think one can pray several hours a day if this is a new experience. Nor can we expect our children to grasp the what, why, when, where, and how of prayer at one go. Since time is at a premium in most families, starting small is the wisest way to begin. This can range from taking five minutes a day for individual prayer to teaching children short mealtime blessings. As we become comfortable with the routine, time parameters widen and memorized prayers expand into spontaneous ones.

Ignore How You Feel

There are a dozen reasons that Ron could draw upon each day to skip his training schedule—it's too hot or cold outside, there's a good show on TV, or he's not in the mood. He rarely, if ever, gives in to any of these. To accomplish his goal, he has to ignore how he feels and, as the commercial advises, "just do it." For him, this is a commitment of time, energy, and dedication. Going about it in haphazard fashion isn't an option.

When I direct retreats, especially for women, I generally hear a number of reasons why it is hard to maintain an active prayer life. We're busy or distracted, the kids need our attention, or our jobs are too demanding. Without diminishing the seriousness of any of these reasons, it usually comes down to setting this as a priority and then making a commitment to it. We find time to tend to all sorts of other things—tuning up a car or getting the kids to band practice. Why is it that, as parents, we can be so quick to let go of the maintenance and renewal of our own souls?

Prayer is more than a nice thing to do. For those who desire a deeper relationship with God, it is essential. While we may shift how, when, or where we pray according to our circumstances, we cannot afford to let go of it because of dry patches or overactive schedules.

Ron may ignore his mental feelings but never dismisses his physical ones. Doing so could lead to long-term injury. In like fashion, we need to be attuned to the wounded parts of ourselves, those most in need of healing. When grieving a loss such as a miscarriage or struggling with betrayal by a friend or relative, we are in a tender space that needs the solace, wisdom, and insight that prayer brings. We ignore such wounds at our own peril, risking a downward plunge into depression and despair. Prayer at such times might lead us to seek the help of a mentor or counselor, or simply open us up to God's quiet presence in the midst of our pain.

Ron often comments on how different one run feels from the next. Sometimes he flies across the trail and other times it is a heavy haul from the first step onward. He stays on course, however, by keeping his eye on the goal. Paul uses a similar analogy in his letter to the Philippians: "This one thing I do: forgetting what lies behind and straining forward to what lies ahead, I press on toward the goal for the prize of the heavenly call of God in Christ Jesus" (Philippians 3:13–14).

With children, who warm to family prayer one day and cool to it the next, this is sage advice. Consistency is the key to guiding children in prayer. In essence, we sometimes have to ignore how they say they feel in order to lay a foundation for their spiritual well-being. This does not mean we fail to respect who they are and what they need. It does mean we hold firm to values that we know will strengthen their hearts and souls for the long haul.

Stay Focused

Coming down the mountain is an equal challenge to going up. Ron has to stay attentive when running downhill lest he take a deadly fall. He repeats a phrase over and over to keep himself in the moment—"Focus and float."

Staying spiritually focused is a necessity when our days are overloaded with detail; otherwise we end up throwing the baby, and a few other essentials, out with the bathwater. Athletes regularly check their heart rates to assess their fitness levels. This is a good idea for parents as well. After all, we don't need to collapse in the kitchen before recognizing signs of physical, mental, and emotional fatigue. We can take our pulse on a daily basis by posing questions that test our spiritual health.

• Am I snapping at those closest to me?

• Am I growing resentful about all I have to do at home, in the workplace, at church, or with my child's school?

• When was the last time I sat still?

• Am I letting my spiritual needs go unmet while taking care of other details in my life and home?

• What effort have I put into praying?

• Do I still have the heart for my faith? My family? My life?

Sometimes the art of asking questions can whack some sense into us and alert us to the need of getting back on track.

When Ron "floats," he is relaxing enough to let gravity do its work and pull him down the mountain. It is an interesting image because floating is usually associated with heading skyward. The key is in lightening up and, through focused awareness, allowing oneself to be carried in the right direction.

The Book of Isaiah contains a beautiful passage that places floating within a context of trust. "Those who wait for the Lord shall renew their strength, they shall mount up with wings like eagles, they shall run and not be weary, they shall walk and not faint" (Isaiah 40:31).

Ron and I chose this passage as a reading for our wedding. Over the years we have talked about being lifted with eagle's wings and given the endurance to carry on while trekking along painful pathways. It is a mysterious process, to be sure. Sometimes, while on the most desolate roads, we have each been given unexpected grace. Perhaps it is because we are most receptive when feeling lost and adrift. This is one of the numerous paradoxes found in Christian belief—finding joy in the midst of sorrow, discovering life after a terrible loss, seeing the clearest when things appear darkest. The force of gravity at such moments draws us deeper into the heart of God.

Being a parent pulls us down some pretty strange roads at times. It is not for the weak-hearted or those afraid to travel without a roadmap. Prayer gives us a spiritual compass, one that leads us on when we are confused, doubtful, or afraid. It also helps to lighten us up, reminding us that our lives, and those of our children, are all part of a much greater picture—one we will only appreciate with a bit of time, distance, and perspective.

Stretch in Different Directions

Before he resumed running Ron set up an intricate regimen of stretching that lasted for months. It is something he maintains faithfully because, as with any form of athleticism, it lowers the risk of injury and promotes flexibility and agility. In addition, he crosstrains by lifting weights and working out on a stair machine as a way to build his strength.

Some of us have cramped up over the years. Maybe it is because religious practices have become habits that no longer make sense to us. Or the movement we have made in prayer has not kept pace with strides we have taken in our family, career, or other aspects of life.

Reading is one way to stretch by opening new pathways to prayer. The possibilities in this direction have never been better. In her book, *Rediscovering the Sacred: Spirituality in America*, Phyllis Tickle described the burgeoning trend in spiritual publishing that was taking place in the nineties. She predicted that it would last well into the twenty-first century, a forecast that has proven to be accurate.

Bookstores that used to carry one shelf of bibles under their religion section now have aisles dedicated to various kinds of fiction and nonfiction material. A plethora of magazines and other periodicals offer articles on the body-soul connection and the how-tos of creating spiritual experiences out of everyday life. The Internet provides access to a wide range of resources, offering everything from e-courses to daily reflections that are deposited directly into one's mailbox.

Another trend is a resurgence of interest in writings by such spiritual giants as John of the Cross, Julian of Norwich, Hildegard of Bingen, and Thomas Merton. The repackaging of their writings into small books of reflections, CDs, and anthologies provides access for modern women and men into the wisdom and traditions of the past. Reading, taking a class, or engaging in a faith-sharing group are all ways to stay spiritually agile.

Being a parent is an experience that stretches us in new and unplanned directions. The birth of a baby with physical or mental disabilities opens up in us a strength we never thought we had. The day a child suddenly starts to read fills us with wonder and awe. The adolescent struggling with issues of identity and acceptance cracks open our hearts in achingly new ways. With each stretch come new glimpses into the mystery of life and our dependence on divine guidance.

Within our families, stretching keeps us resilient. When we relinquish rigid expectations of prayer, we can embrace a spirituality that allows us to go with the flow of life. Flexibility then becomes the counterpoint to consistency, giving rise to possibility, surprise, and spontaneity.

Let Go

Ron did make it up and down Pikes Peak, finishing the marathon in seventh place overall and second in his age group. It was a fantastic moment for him and for all of us who cheered him on. The following year he competed in the Ascent, a race to the top of the mountain, hoping to beat or come close to the age group record. While he placed first in his age group, his time was ten minutes slower than he hoped. Even though I considered it another triumph, he was disappointed.

Running is a risky endeavor. One twist of the ankle and it is all over. A slight increase in temperature or humidity slows everyone down and throws all times off course. Ron is a seasoned runner. While the disappointment over his finish at the Ascent was hard, he is aware that this is part of the risk. Setbacks are just that. He moves on and continues to see each part of the process as essential—from the stretching to the finish line. While he has drawn upon conventional wisdom in his day-to-day discipline, he has also crafted a plan that works for him. That's what makes his running more than a physical workout; it is a soulful experience.

One of my friends told me about the effort she put into learning about a particular form of prayer, one that required a lot of time, attentiveness, and an ability to be still. After several frustrated attempts at making it a regular practice, she began to berate herself over what she perceived was a failure in making it work. A monk whom she had sought for spiritual guidance gave her some advice. "Don't pray what you can't; pray what you can."

Praying what we can means to stop heaping "shoulds" upon ourselves. Traditional forms of prayer contain much wisdom. I hope that I have conveyed some of it in this book. Each of us has to run our own race, however, by choosing the style, form, and means of prayer that match our preferences, needs, interests, longings, and flow of life. Letting go of expectations about how we *should* be praying allows us to pray what we *can* be praying.

Guiding children in prayer also takes a relinquishment of expectations. It is, at best, a seed-planting process. We may never find out what took root and eventually blossomed inside of them. Even when they rebel, resist, and retreat down paths that are far from our choosing, we can hope that something was rooted in them. We cannot ensure that they will have faith, but we won't give up on their spirits. And, as we become more seasoned in our roles as parents, we understand that we can let them go and trust that they are being watched over by a God who loves them far more than we do.

Staying Power

After the September 11 attack on the World Trade Center, there were a number of theories put forth about why the buildings collapsed in the manner that they did. One of these held that the fire, intensified by the jet fuel, reached temperatures that melted the inner core of the structure. The center could not hold.

Whenever I study the photograph of our family sitting together in the hotel lobby months before the attack, I think of the unexpected events and unsettling experiences that have peppered our lives. Some have been jarring enough to almost knock us off our foundations. My son's words about being a strong family then come back to me. The center—which is love—does hold, and it only grows stronger with time.

As a parent, I honestly don't know how I would have made it to that point and beyond it without the strength, assurance, and peace that prayer has brought me. It has given me insight when everything seemed murky and kept me steady when the ground beneath me shifted. It helped me forgive when I felt betrayed and to move on when I was tempted to wallow in self-pity.

Prayer has lifted my heart and brought me to tears. It has driven me to my knees and compelled me to dance. It is the best way I know to meet the challenge and cherish the joy that being a parent is all about.

Resources for Prayer

For Parents: Reflections and Books on Spirituality and Prayer

Cox, Harvey. *Common Prayers: Faith, Family, and a Christian's Journey Through the Jewish Year.* New York: Houghton Mifflin Company, 2000.

Davis, Patricia H. *Beyond Nice: The Spiritual Wisdom of Adolescent Girls.* Minneapolis: Augsberg Fortress, 2001.

Groome, Thomas H. *What Makes Us Catholic: Eight Gifts for Life.* New York: HarperCollins, 2002.

Hanh, Thich Nhat. *The Miracle of Mindfulness: A Manual on Meditation.* Boston: Beacon Press, 1975.

Harris, Maria. *Dance of the Spirit: The Seven Steps of Women's Spirituality.* New York: Bantam Books, 1989.

Hays, Edward M. *Pray All Ways.* Notre Dame, IN: Ave Maria Press/Forest of Peace Books, 1981.

Hart, Patrick and Jonathan Montaldo, eds. *The Intimate Merton: His Life from His Journals.* New York: HarperCollins Publishers, Inc., 1999.

Moore, Thomas. *Care of the Soul.* New York: HarperCollins, 1992.

Muller, Wayne. *Learning to Pray.* New York: Bantam Dell, 2003

Mundy, Linus. *The Complete Guide to Prayer-Walking.* New York: The Crossroad Publishing Company, 1996.

Nouwen, Henri. *The Inner Voice of Love: A Journey from Anguish to Freedom.* New York: Image Books, 1998.

———. *The Return of the Prodigal Son: A Story of Homecoming.* New York: Image Books, 1992.

Remen, Rachel Naomi. *My Grandfather's Blessings: Stories of Strength, Refuge, and Belonging.* New York: Riverhead Books, 2000.

Rolheiser, Ronald. *The Holy Longing: The Search for A Christian Spirituality.* New York: Doubleday, 1999.

Rupp, Joyce. P*raying Our Goodbyes.* Notre Dame, IN: Ave Maria Press, 1983.

Wolfe, Gregory and Suzanne M. Wolfe. *Circle of Grace.* New York: Ballantine Books, 2000.

Prayers and Prayer Ideas for Families

Anglund, Joan Walsh. *A Little Book of Poems and Prayers.* New York: Simon and Schuster Books for Young Readers, 1989.

Berger, Alison. *Jesus, Teach Me to Pray: A Catholic Child's Prayerbook.* Mystic, CT: Twenty-Third Publications, 1999.

Chesto, Kathleen O'Connell. *Family Prayer for Family Times.* Mystic, CT: Twenty Third Publications, 1995.

Costello, Gwen. *Blessed Are You: A Prayerbook for Catholics.* Mystic, CT: Twenty Third Publications, 2003.

Curran, Dolores. *Dolores Curran on Family Prayer.* Mystic, CT: Twenty Third Publications, 1997.

Denham, Joyce. *A Child's Book of Celtic Prayers.* Chicago: Loyola Press, 1998.

Duncan, Geoffrey, ed. *600 Blessings and Prayers from Around the World.* Mystic, CT: Twenty Third Publications, 2001.

Edelman, Marian Wright. *Guide My Feet: Prayers and Meditations for Our Children.* Boston: Beacon Press, 1995.

Hays, Edward M. *Prayers for the Domestic Church.* Notre Dame, IN: Ave Maria Press/Forest of Peace Books, 1979.

———. *Prayers for a Planetary Pilgrim.* Notre Dame, IN: Ave Maria Press/Forest of Peace Books, 1988.

Prayers and Practices for Young Catholics. New York: William H. Sadlier, Inc., 1997.

Rathschmidt, Jack and Gaynell Bordes Cronin. *Rituals for Home and Parish.* Mahwah, NJ: Paulist Press, 1996.